ELEPHANT ENGINE HIGH DIVE REVIVAL

CRISTIN O'KEEFE APTOWICZ
ROGER BONAIR-AGARD
DERRICK C. BROWN
BRIAN S. ELLIS
SHIRA ERLICHMAN
ANDREA GIBSON
MIKE MCGEE
ANIS MOJGANI
MINDY NETTIFEE
SHAPPY SEASHOLTZ
SONYA RENEE TAYLOR
ROBBIE Q. TELFER
BUDDY WAKEFIELD
KIT WALLACH

A Write Bloody Book
Long Beach. CA USA

Elephant Engine High Dive Revival

Write Bloody Publishing ©2009.
1ˢᵗ printing.
Printed in LONG BEACH, CA USA

Elephant Engine High Dive Revival Copyright 2009.
All Rights Reserved.

Published by Write Bloody Publishing.

Printed in Long Beach, CA USA.

Cover Art by Anis Mojgani
Cover Design by Josh Grieve
Interior Layout by Lea C. Deschenes
Edited by Derrick Brown & Robbie Q. Telfer
Type set in Helvetica Neue and Bell MT

To contact the authors, send an email to writebloody@gmail.com

WRITE BLOODY PUBLISHING
LONG BEACH, CA

ELEPHANT ENGINE HIGH DIVE REVIVAL

CRISTIN O'KEEFE APTOWICZ

JUNKYARD GHOST REVIVAL

It was October, and New England was stupid with beauty.
Anis obsessively took out-of-focus photos of it streaming
by our van window, all blurry red-gold-orange. The four
of us—me, Anis, Buddy, and Derrick—were old enough not
to lose our shit when Anis left the cash box in a hotel room
in Amherst, but still young enough to be shameless suckers
for roadside stands and ambitiously pretty waitresses.
I always thought on tours like this, I'd blow out my voice
by the third day, but I was wrong. I was right, however,
about bringing Presidential flash cards, lots of warm socks
and extra toothpaste. I was the only one in the van not nursing
a broken heart, and consequently, I made the worst DJ.
The world's largest and smallest hamburgers can be found
at the same diner in Pennsylvania in a town which also claims
to have a haunted corn maze and the state's best Shoofly pie.
We had to keep driving, though. The one day we had off was
spent in Maine: first, at an antiques shop selling dusty books
and tiny pewter birds we later learned were salt shakers;
and after, at a lobster shack so close to the ocean, the wind
dried the butter to our chins before the napkins had a chance.
Every other night, we stomped on the hardwood, pulled books
out of boxes, then stuffed them right back in, we'd flopped down
on a series of different empty beds. But sometimes in between,
we'd marvel at the sky from the parking lot: the moon doing
its usual magic, the stars poking through the clouds, the air fresh
and slick and hopeful; tomorrow, not slowing down for a second.

BE PREPARED

When the black plague hit the Saxon army in the 1340's,
they didn't let this stop them. Instead they catapulted
the diseased corpses of their fellow soldiers directly
into the enemy camp. It worked. Within a year, half
of Scotland was dead. Half the Saxons were dead too,
but at least, they knew how to put their dead to work.

In the 1930's, in the middle of legendary circus tent fire
which would swallow almost two hundred people, a little boy
with a club foot remembered his boy scout pen knife
and sliced a hole through the tent large enough for him
and three hundred other strangers to fit through. He thought this
would make people see past his disability. The next day,
the headline read: *Boy with Club Foot Saves Hundreds.*

In 2008, the U.S. National Parks Service reported
a significant uptick in suicides within their parks.
I guess they want to die someplace beautiful, said
the parks spokesman, but this is not the answer.
The Grand Canyon claims the most suicides by far
and park rangers are now instructed to look out
for signs: notes taped to steering wheels; weeping;
the lone person staring too long into the abyss.

In 2009, I stare into the abyss of another poem,
struggling hard not to include you. Obviously,

it fails when, in the last stanza, you appear,
out of nowhere, mute, nodding your woolly head.
Look, I have no dead Saxon to throw at you,
no knife to slice through your lingering everything.
I only have this poem, the one I am taping
to the steering wheel of page, swearing to you
I'm not lonely, that I don't miss you at all, that
I was grateful when silence enveloped us both,
happy that if the "us" we became had to die,
at least it would be someplace beautiful.

DRUNK BOYFRIEND AT THE POETRY READING

Fidgeting at the bar, he groans,
This is more boring than church, and
I'm allowed to drink margaritas here.

At the same time, the poet on stage tells us
that his hands aren't hands; that his hands
are, in fact, the echoes of child's silent tears.

Furthermore, the poet on stage tells us,
his tongue isn't a tongue; it's a road even
the Aztec warriors are afraid to tread.

Meanwhile, my drunk partner at the bar
tells me that his balls aren't balls, but
are actually bear's feet surgically

attached to his dick to look like balls,
and oh yeah, his dick is a highway, and
people want to ride it all night long.

I give the bartender a sign meaning
cut him off, while he gives a sign meaning
two more shots. Guess who wins?

At home, I make him eat a sandwich
and drink two tall tumblers of water while

I try to get some writing done. *I think*

we are so great, he says, *I'm serious.*
I know, I answer. *Hey, hey,* he whispers.
I'm sorry I didn't have a better time

at the reading. That's okay, I say,
maybe next time. *Hey, hey, he whispers.*
What did I say my balls were again?

Bear paws, I reply. *Oh man, that's*
priceless. It's funny because it's true!
Write that down. Stop what you're

doing and write that down. It's gold.
And if you don't use it in a poem,
let me know, cause if you don't, I will.

NOT AS SMART AS I THINK I AM

I know that the "57" in Heinz 57 refers to the number
of pickles that the company used to sell, and that
graham crackers and corn flakes were originally
created to prevent masturbation, but I can't tell you
the difference between a seal and sea lion. Or
the difference between an alligator and a crocodile,
though I think it has to do something with the shape
of their snouts. Pumas and leopards are the same cats
with different colored coats, and something called
"the wingless fly" lives in Antarctica, but I only
know this because I saw it on a PBS kid's show once,
and also, I had to google the spelling of Antarctica
because my computer dictionary told me I wasn't
even close. You know, they say that there is a part
of the human chest that if you strike it hard enough,
it makes the person's heart explode. This sounds like
such a lie that I have to believe it's the truth. If I were
science, I'd never tell anyone where this place is.
If I were science, I'd have named this place after you.

ROGER BONAIR-AGARD

FABLE TOWARDS BECOMING A POET

On a morning when he walked to school down the main road
across the lush botanical gardens, his top button undone
so he could hear the humming in his own chest, mimic
the mad fluster of the birds' wings, he understood himself
immediately in possession of a history he did not yet understand.
The savannah lay ahead, with its heady aromas of cut grass
and bush bug, morning sun and coconut water, and the Ben Gay
remnants from the previous evening's matches he swore you could
still smell if you crossed the savannah walking between
        the goal posts.
It wasn't that he didn't know exactly what the history was.
        It was only
too obvious, the massive acres of savannah that used to be
        crop, the big
houses on one side, the opposite still, even today a massive circular
ghetto of previous barrack yards, from the tip of Belmont Circular
Road to Jerningham Avenue. It was that some days he thought he
smelled blood. And of course he would have dismissed it, as part
of the remnants from the rugby games or the hostility of a delivery
from one of the cricket matches on the unreliable and
        unruly wickets
placed helter skelter throughout; tiny band-aids on the savannah's
weathered face. But the blood smell was too strong in the
        wind, the
savannah too broad for it to be brought from somewhere
        without it.

Besides, he felt he could smell steel too, in that way that when the
cutlass whistles down—near, at you, or by your own hand, all your
nerves concentrate so thoroughly as to fan themselves throughout
the senses so that what is seen or heard is keenly felt,
        tickles the nostrils
too—and so he smelled the steel.

It was why he was always late for school, so much so that
        the school
began a minor investigation into the boy's habits, and his mother
wondered if the boy had taken to drugs, and grown-ups on their
way to work would report that the boy had been seen
        idling on his way
to school, not even hustling even though it was past seven-
        thirty, always
trying to look like a saga-boy, top button undone and
        sauntering, like
he didn't know he had a scholarship to go and try to get. But, the
boy was not indolent. He was forever distracted by that wind, the
entire Caribbean archipelago it seemed assailing him from
        whatever
died there amongst the once-canes of the Queen Park Savannah,
whatever still groaned under a boot heel, so he had to sit
        down sometimes
with a snow cone (extra syrup, condensed milk), just to
        measure the
seppy, try to figure out what ghost was calling to him,
        from the sand track,
from the North Stand, from the Hollows where even he himself

from time to time might be able to beg a little pull-tongue
      and feel-up
from a girl, and so he studied the bougainvillea, the
      hibiscus, the heliconia
and dappled crocus leaf. He studied the Ti-Marie and the
      pond water,
the rusted band shell and the cracks in the pavement
      concrete that ringed
the whole rigamarole.

By the time he sat down for the first class then, of course
      he was tired.
Didn't matter the thermos of coffee he pulled out of his
      bag, he was
often asleep in less than half hour. Didn't matter the
      subject either,
Latin or French, Integrated Science or Economics, his friends
had to wake him several times a day—or they didn't. He had
other worlds exploring, other histories being invented and
      dreamed
up. Even then, this teacher or that performing away at the front
of the room, voices still kept calling through the Main Building
jalousies, an efficient breeze coming from the Belmont barrack
yards that now housed Casablanca or Renegades, through to bring
him their sermons or continue on toward the Ministry in
      the West.
This is what he remembered when years later, he was
      asked why he
couldn't stay up in class, that Africans were always bringing him
stories to tell, desperate ones, begging him for a history here,

a memory there. They would leave him with names of rivers
he couldn't understand why he knew, or the locations of lost
things. Later when he stopped writing for seven years, they would
come and take back things from him, small things, jewelry
    and money
to remind him, how he had come to know anything at all.
    He was lucky
they ever came back and told him anything, insistent ancestors
they were. It meant he was always going to be late somewhere,
always hearing something nobody else heard, always
    catching a whiff
of something nobody had lit. He was never going to be on time
and sometimes when he was in his liquors, he left the
    gathered anyway,
but it meant that whenever he returned, he was always
    going to have
something to share.

FIRST GOAL

You've been a god ever since
that first day; the initial catechism
of grass and sweat, the mercurial ball
arriving on the inside of the instep—a gift,
and one time your body was a long, tense rod
of give and want—you turned—the tug
on your shirt—the grunts of the defender,
nothing short of prayer, and you swore
you could smell the rind of cologne he used,
the dirt underneath the fresh cut grass,
the supple, polished leather of your own
cleats—so clear and deft your ghost dance,
and the defender straining against your forearm
was the wind in Ulysses's sails, so that you pushed
on the ball, now on your foot as if attached there
with string, and the crowd's rising regalia, your own
thighs taut as first sex, every sinew a gallantry
of power and feint—you never forget
the hot weight of the ball leaving your foot,
the unloosed tourniquet of your body
sending it goalward, the thick cotton
of the net an everlasting seine
as it undulated like a stingray—like a prostrating
towards you. You can almost swear you remember
what the air sounded like. The sun was your angel—
your first goal scored—you are fire, you are joy, your body
is a hymn, you are living, you are weeping. You are God.

GULF

We crossed the gulf in a blue rowboat,
Hayden swimming the pitch blue seas
beside us. We whispered the count as we slid
the boats into the surf and roared it loud
as we hit the choppy Paria the constellations
crisp as music in the skies above us
leaning into the water's weight with every
grunt—*stroke stroke stroke stroke*
the chant now a kind of prayer ecstatic
immersion of young boys into the black deep
on our way to the Guayagayare caves and
the deep cold pools inside them.

Begin again. Once or twice when I was twelve,
I dared enough to join the other boys
in theft of the boats so I could say I was there.
I was mortally afraid but grabbed
the oars and joined too in the shouting.
I wanted to be remembered, to be holy
there in the silent midnight waking
skulking quiet as ninjas into open ocean
braving jellyfish drowning and bigger
vessels just to belong, which is to say
I had not yet proven myself, and was
too afraid to decline the invitation.

We clambered over the limestone
to the top of the caves and jumped
through the hole one by one to fall thirty
feet through blackness to the unexpected
splash at the bottom. In time I'd come
to understand risk to be much like this
the heart rising through the throat
the body combed through and through
by an enveloping blackness every second
of the plunge a comfort of chanting start
receding in a ring above the body a boat
the silent pool beneath a welcoming death.

AMERICA, AMERICA, A SONG REMEMBERING

(after Ernest Bloch's Sonata for violin and piano)

Wade in the water, wade in the water children
Wade in the water. I'm gonna trouble the water. . . .
                          American Negro spiritual

What does it mean when a song remembers,
when a negro spiritual buries itself
like a thunder inside an evening?
What does it mean if the thunder shows
and proves inside a tune, claps its hands
points its way north?

All morning this weather of music
all these barometers alive at the sonata's
center, so the wood and iron become bells,
fists; so the strings are an immigration
of wind, so desperate, the song calls
and calls the listener forward, calls
and calls to his past, impels him north,
past field and windmill, past the cock-sure
weather-vanes, past any line that would drag
him too far back. Listen, let's be clear—the song

is a brilliant scrawling from the fist of an infant
country who swears it hears its mother's wailing
through the long, enduring night, who hears its mother's

own reaching into the old country beyond the seas—
the remembering so violent, it creaks like a rusted
hinge and makes thunder in the violet night,
the angels racing around to corral the dreams
back into the infant's palms, his railroad-tight
limbs, his colicky and wheezing chest.

What does it remember when a song remembers
in several directions at once, when the song
is a head-scarved black woman, when the song
raises its head from the shtetls, when the song
is Andalusian, when the song knows desert,
plough and tundra, when the song is wading
into an ocean to call several continents at once,
when the song is frantic with its want, when the song
is mourning, mourning, and remembering,
because the song is water and the water is a planet
of anguish and recollection, so the song calls to it
as to a graveyard at midnight.

This is where the song recognizes the flowers
in the field, even the ones choking
the headstones. The song calls each one
by name and medicinal purpose. The song
after all, is not crossing without its secrets
of poultice and tea, without something to occasionally
press to the belly of the sick infant. The song has been
here so long, it know things it shouldn't. No wonder
the immigrant song drags itself one coast to the next
on the rails of an old negro spiritual. It is racking

the ribcage of the infant country, forcing the lullabies
of all the mothers made to grieve the deaths
of children—*Oh God* they wail. *Oh God* they cry
out—*hide my babies from this lash, take them across
your rivers. Take them to a promised land.*

DERRICK C. BROWN

JAPANESE PAPER

1.
The girl with the engine-black painted nails and legal drinking age
who hates the dog dying in her purse
needs me.

The business loafers,
cold water fountain drippings on their shirt.
Dehydrated faces with deep woeful lines like
bathroom stall wall knife graffiti.
They need me.

The foreign faces in bad sandals and heavy smiles,
lost and smelling like a high school locker rag.
They need me too.

You can spot the smokers coming off the plane.
One hand with carry-on bag, the other balled tight
as a ballerina's hair bun.

In the summer I sold lighters
at the end of the baggage claim for extra cash.
I stood with a sign that said "The lighter at the end of the tunnel."

I scored them from security for the departing flights.
I would sell them for pure profit, pulling about 130 bucks a day.
People often told me they loved me.

Pats on the back.

I knew the imperfect desperate look,
the ragged and provoked look.
They needed me.

2.
There was one woman. Margaret.
The faint lemon grove.
and basil in her hair, rosemary breath.
A face full of traveler's sheen, heading nowhere in particular,
just getting away.

My hands smell of butane and I miss her classic smoke.
I think of her when I am holding still.

So many years before
I was tearing through horndog streets,
walking like a machete
through the lush envy of other men.
She asked for a light.

                                        Her words
      came like a pre-monsoon breeze
                            trembling across
    Japanese paper. "Hello, delicate," she said.
I followed Margaret.
How it started is not as sweet as what we came to be.

3.
We were in the dumbest seasonal love.

We were laughing merlot up,
throwing bottles into the rafters,
wine narcotics dripping upon our skin
desire hoarse
an aurora parade
the body astonished.

For Halloween, you dressed as Thanksgiving.
I dressed as an "in-flight movie"
and bored you into my arms.

One evening I said, Margaret, every day, strangers tell me
     they love me.
I know that they don't really love me; they love what I do.
I like it no matter the intention.
We've spent months together
and you have never said that you love me. I want to see
     what it does.
I want to see if I twitch.

She said, "*I love what you do to me.*"

I love what you do, too, Margaret.

The best relationships
fade out
and you're not even sure
when it ended.

4.
Back in my sweet spot by the baggage carousel,
a pink suitcase.
I stare at it for too long and now I see a vision of a plane,
mid-flight, splitting
like the black seam of your stungun-stockings:

luggage and lingerie fall to the earth
children grab umbrellas
as the sky roars down high heels, slinky neckties and
panties, panties. . . .
panties panties panties. . . .

No one survives but everyone enjoys the ride
when they figure out how to stop screaming.

I don't think about what they lost.
I think, there go my customers.
There go the people that kept me alive.
I wonder if, on certain doomed flights,
people get that tingle that something isn't right
but you hope you are wrong and close your eyes
and wait.

I snap from the daydream.

5.
I see the escalator bringing travelers down to no waiting party
and I am there with my box of colors and sign.

I look at the screen of arrivals
and I see Margaret's home phone,
her bra size, her birthday in the numbers.

A man with his tie flipped behind his neck lines up to buy a
    lighter and says,
"Oh, buddy, you just saved my life. "

Two dollars, please.

"I am surprised no one busts ya. Selling back to people
something taken away from them is kinda strange, huh?"

I am restoring the balance.

"You savin' up for vacation?"

I am saving up to buy a plane ticket. Nowhere special. Two dollars.

He says "You have no idea how thankful I am for this."

I say, I have an idea.

He rummages for a minute,
checking to see which lighter has the most fuel in it until
    his eyes widen.
"Hey, this is my lighter. I bought it in Texas.
This is the lighter they made me get rid of. What a trip.
I drew my initials on the bottom. See. D.G. I can have it, right?"

Sure, but there is a resurrection fee.

"How much?"

Two dollars.

Bags and bags coming down the carousel,
Endless.
Some never get picked up.

AMBIEN

They found daisies growing in Jonestown
where the bodies and grape punch
laid in the pavilion 30 years later.

Hyacinth Thrash, 76, was there that day
slept through it all
and decided to live.

The feeling washing over her
as she tried to remember the dream
she had before waking to the sight
of everyone she loved, gone.

I want to sleep that hard tonight
with the world
convulsing around me.

IF YOU BUY AN OLD POLYGRAPH AT A SWAP MEET, DO NOT BREAK IT OUT AT A PARTY

When I first brought the thing home
I had no idea it would change me for the better.
Honesty is a wide shot of a movie lot.

Now, I cannot trust lovers or anyone with curly hair.
The clerk at the supermarket wants my life.
The hairdresser keeps looking at my neck
and then the scissors
and then my neck.
I don't trust you. Your pants are baggy.
You've got choking hands.
All dresses are fingerprint recording devices.
I don't trust your painted face.
I don't like that you keep looking down or that your eyes
    shift into neutral. . . .
like a dying man's. . . .
as a dying man's.

How do you know what is honest anymore?
Because your snotty toddler is not the most adorable thing
    in the world?
Because the cops don't actually care if you have a nice day?
Because you are not the world's best grandma and didn't
    even apply in time?
Because that chocolate is not to die for unless you were a dog

and then you'd just be a dead dog?
Because I am still alive and death did not do us part?

Trust the machine.
You can trust something without a heartbeat.

Everyone practiced cheating the machine
through breathing techniques,
biting of the tongue,
thumbtacks
and various squeezing of butt muscles.

It didn't matter.

"Have you ever wanted someone more than me?"
"Have you ever lied to me?"

The slightest pause means gather the jackets.
Everything honest ends in silence.

GROCERY LIST

Be more forgiving.
Substitute "goodbye" for "I like your face."
Spend two nights a week not drinking to forget.
Listen to your body.
Listen to someone else's body.
Get limber.
Don't dog yourself to feel humble. It never works.
Lift others up onto your back until you are sore.
Write for yourself a movie that doesn't end.
Eat a churro slowly.
Kiss your mother on the cheek and don't miss.
Remember that now is barely now. It will soon be back
    then. Stop.
Don't text anyone while talking with anyone.
Finish everything.
Get Milk.

BRIAN S. ELLIS

GRACIOUS UNEMPLOYMENT

Last night, between rereading
the Wikipedia entry on Amelia Earhart
and drinking that warm forty
my roommate's friend left behind two days ago
I made a facebook profile for my cat!

Good Morning Eleven Thirty!
I am Unemployed!
Gracious unemployment, so eager
to welcome me into the boozy mire of you
Time is lying incapacitated at your feet
like a blind man you hit in the face with a crowbar
His teeth: splashing and bouncing across
the days of the week, like the bathroom walls
of a strip club in New Jersey

How we come to mark our days
by the accumulation of small, broken promises
I'm going to bring in that application to popcorn galaxy
after the weekend, it actually would be really good for me
How easy it is to mistake survival for living
How quickly we become house pets
On Saturday I spent six hours just . . . flopping around
like a diseased turtle

Every morning the carpet tries
to dupe me into becoming a part of it
Without work, my work has become

being anything but a hallway
My work is to keep my home
from transforming into anything else

Suns and moons disappear behind buzzing monitors
The names of dead gods
splinter under the weight of motionlessness
while hunger looms like the opposite of a birthday

Alone, I forced to fashion purpose
without a punch-clock
or push-broom dreams
renaming days and hours
based upon the frequency of showers and masturbating

There is so much poverty inside of me
Its language is fear
Fear's alphabet is song of paralysis
from within paralysis I will learn
what the burn of muscle is willing to live for
I must climb out the well of myself myself
I must learn how to wear my name unseen

WHY I DO NOT PICK UP THE PHONE

My father bellowed from across the house
for me to pick up the phone
It was never for me

When telephone numbers still meant
a place on the map
the voices on the other end
wanted to know if my father was home
Cordially at first, and then,
with greater and greater venom
Credit card companies, collection agencies,
the IRS. Their voices were starched white
Ironed. You could hear their closely
cropped haircut, the fluoride rinse

The same customer service representatives
would keep calling back
trying to outwit a nine-year-old
burgeoning storyteller
They would grow angry, then solemn
claiming to know more about my family than I did
As I tried to hide all over my father in my voice

I'm still holding him in here

I pretended to be everything that I am not:
stupid, obedient, and shocked
by the severity of adults

I left everything I wanted to tell them
stranded in my bookbag-sized chest

I hate your teeth
Your college education
Your faith in this game of money
That you have no idea that
it will one day turn on you, too
and it will still mean nothing

Winning and Losing are two words that both mean loneliness

You're breaking my father's heart
and you don't have to be here when it happens
He used to be one of you

To this day, I still call him
my father
To this day, I'm still surprised when the phone is for me

WE KNOW WHO WE ARE NOW

New England boys can get drunk on sunlight alone
so when we do drink,
things get special
That spring it rained for two weeks unrelenting
My best friend Adam had parted ways
with his seven-year sweetheart
and he wanted me to teach him
to like whiskey so we drank on our back porch
and watched commitment fall out of the sky
Twenty-three years old and still alive
I was giddy for my lack of homelessness
but Adam still hadn't been convinced about roofs
he told me about the dreams he had
about his unknown father
the inheritance of mystery and addiction

Twenty-three years old and out of weed
we started making phone calls
Next thing you know
we're sprinting to Allston in a downpour
shouting and shaking strangers' hands
giving away cigarettes and laughing
about the meaninglessness of the days of the week

The Garden of Eden was never a physical place
Eden is still present in the eyes

of every animal except one
Even on some of the most inconsequential nights
the naked human launches out of the animal in us
into a new way of seeing
spastic and ranting, running through the rain
to smoke one bowl
Adam and I, we knew who we were now:
Inebriated and moralistic, immune to media
Disbelievers of binary opposition
The first last survivors of the twentieth century

The founding fathers were not much more
than a pack of drunk teenagers
with ideas louder than their mouths
dashing through the streets of Boston
trying to stitch together a patchwork Utopia
with everything they could steal

Utopia is as far from Eden as one can travel
but we can run there
on the endless energy of the effortless
Harvard Avenue gulped as slick
as the curtain of possibility
under the heavy drumroll of our chattering youth

The fabric of paradise is a cloak of inhumanity
Happiness has never saved anyone's life
but still, we lift our hearts to the rain
asking to know more
Our origin is not in the clay

and not in the rib
Our origin is in the moment of the bite
Because we are made of knowledge

That night, Adam and I had an idea
We're going to start a new nation
We're going to call it America
Because Utopia is not enough
Because if the most deadly century
of all time did not destroy us
then nothing will
And because Thomas Jefferson
ain't got shit on my lyrics

LETTER FROM MY VOICE

Dear Brian Stephen Ellis,

Stop Being Afraid Of The World

        Sincerely,

        Your Voice

P.S. Stop blaming things on the insects
Stop blaming things on the scathing eyes of men
Stop blaming things on sand, and money and the sun
Remember that your stomach is outside of your body
and your heart is just mystery waiting to become color
You have tried to hide me in the paper sack of your intestines
in the gambleshiver fist of your liver
You have tried to hide me in your eyes
the alarm clocks your mother built from snow globes and
     owl feathers
Instead, I learned to scream from your tear-ducts

I will abuse you until you claim me
Have you seen the insides of your lungs lately?
They're covered in bruises
I've been ripping nightmares out through your larynx
like tearing sheets of wool from your ventricles

Now, you cough up mobiles of twilight

Brian—your past is a motel
every muscle in your body a room
Hidden behind those doors are boys
you should have evicted long ago
the teenager that let life
slip through knuckle-heavy fingers
the screaming adolescent that
punches himself in the night
the grade-school insomniac
with tear and snot scarred face
the little boy who begged god
to take his imagination away
so he could finally sleep
I never fit inside of those children
Do not let the knife wound
of your caesarian birth chase you to the grave

When you speak,
echo every gulp of oxygen
ancestor sacrificed to bring you to life
When you speak lift the ships of ghosts
in your veins into the air
When you speak make the bell
of your throat the champion of blisters

Do not let the muscle shiners, and the pollen lipped
convince you that you are small
Do not let the greedtarians and the cocksafe

look down their easy answers at you
When you speak,
make the billows of your lungs
the mouth of the Atlantic
When you speak, whip your crooked teeth
into a savage halo
Bravery will never belong to the beautiful
Remember that you are a conduit of the wind
and admit to me that you can fly

I am the only thing you will ever truly own
I am your voice
and I am your only chance at freedom

SHIRA ERLICHMAN

ALL COMPETITIVE FOR SPEED TRAIN FUNDING

The National Meeting was becoming rowdy. "If we have the speed
train, we will never have to walk again," said a representative
from Minnesota, causing a ripple of affirmations, including
vigorous nods. "Imagine," said New Hampshire to a packed room
of people who loved the word imagine, "whisking through towns
at speeds over one hundred miles an hour, walking only a few steps
to public transportation and ending up just blocks from
        your destination."
"It could solve crime!" shouted a voice that couldn't be anchored.
New Jersey rose with solemnity, "Imagine," (there it was again)
"at one hundred miles per hour, we could clothe the needy,
        teach our toddlers to read,
and plug the hole in the economy." New York jumped out
        of its seat,
"At one hundred miles per hour, we could teach algebra to those
not mathematically inclined." New York sat down, case made.
"Industry, the magnetic field, the Constitution," said Rhode Island.
The whole Northeast was getting real revved up. "I
        motion to motion
for a vote on which state gets the first installment," said California,
"Whoever motions to motion, say aye." "Aye!" a chorus of
        statesmen
and stateswomen clattered back like beautiful bells. What I
        would have given
to be a beautiful bell; but I didn't even know how I got here.
I looked down at my name tag: Sydney Wilds, Vermont.
No one in Vermont even wanted the speed train. I had to

raise my own funds
to get here. And why did I even want the train? Attention?
   Flowers? Industry?
"Wait," I said, "the voice in me says speak up." Everyone
   turned around to face me.
This was clearly a place where inner voices were respected.
I was standing on legs of liquid, dizzy. As I spoke the most
   vivid articulation
of my fears, I saw comets, as frightening as they were elegant,
weaving in and out of the crowd. The room was silent in
   my gentle clutch.
I began my ending, quieting down so as to intensify the
   heat of the room.
"I like to walk," I said, "I like crime. I love that the needy
constantly need; they are the only ones still human among us
Technicolor angels. If we teach the toddlers to read, they will
raid us for answers we don't have too soon. We should hold off
as long as possible from even teaching them to speak." Then
I brought it down to a barely audible sound, thin as steam.
"I like the hole in the economy. I like holes in general.
Their emptiness gives them purpose. Algebra," I laughed here,
with a touch of cruelty. "It is one of my most passionate
concerns. I am the maestro of my household. As for those not
mathematically inclined, my husband is one of them.
If the speed train taught him algebraic wisdom, the delicate math
inherent to our relationship would tilt, causing an inevitable
divorce." The crowd was rapt, caught in a spider web of anguish
and awe. "Flowers." I said. That was all it took. They
couldn't help but murmur to one another. A sea of humans
whispering "flowers" and all that would be destroyed
would not be.

AND YET, BEING, I WRITE A POEM, THOUGH

Today don't want to write a poem, though
I want to. And I want the world goned. And want
to offer myself this world. And want to throw bricks at
word midnight. And want to offer myself this world
too blue black to be real, and watch it be. Throw bricks at
word midnight, to feed hours flesh too blue black to be
real, being and being yet and yet I watch it. Want,
feed, hours pass my flesh, I explain myself to dogs,
who need none explaining, and yet, what song here.
I explain to dogs myself who need no explaining, whistle
myself onto bus like a sunrise over nowhere, what song here,
bellow, trumpet-headed street-walkers, whoa me open.
Whistle myself onto bus brushing past so many suns.
Lonely is one too many syllables for daylight, bellow,
trumpet-heads, street-walkers, whoa me open like a sack
of flour exploding. Daylight is one too many syllables for
lonely, and I don't want quite to quit, but like a sack of flour,
explode to grow wings. And I don't want quite to quit
but, want the goned world to grow wings. Today don't
want to grow wings though, explode, or talk back.
And yet, being, I write a poem, though.

ON THE SIDE OF THE ROAD, PURGATORY, MASSACHUSETTS

Is it a fish tank or is it a balloon, the girl with the bloody stump
says to herself, staring at the plastic bag in the puddle. I like your
fist, says the old lady passing her, pointing to the bloody stump.
The girl is small, and goat-like, and can't manage the five words
she wishes to say most: It is not a fist. And anyways, the lady
is gone. She is half an hour ahead of herself, always. She is
already doing the dishes in the next town over, rubbing her thighs
together while soap bubbles fly and pop. Rub, rubbing. In
    the friction of it,
caught and wet in that triangle of tangles, she imagines
    her husband's fingers,
pulling out the slow ribbon of her incoming orgasm. The girl
with the bloody stump knows the scent on the wind is dish-bleach
and cum. She holds her radiant rose of a non-fist up to the light
to examine the damage. There is a bone sticking out. She begins
to feel immense pity for her twelve-string guitar, which will never
again know the strum-strum of her hummingbird right
    hand. Am I dead?
It is winter, so she breathes out, to test it. A yellow dog trots by.
She reaches out to him with the stump. The dog shows his teeth.
It is a fury: the scream coming from her own throat, the
    ghost-recognition
in the dog's eyes, the crowd that does nothing. She steps back,
putting her good hand out, so as to appease the dog. He
    seems pleased enough

so he disappears. Perhaps he has become a mountain. The
    mountain
in the distance does seem dog-like. It is true: it is the most
    dog-like mountain
anyone has ever seen. There is a river in you, a baby says
    to her as he is
strolled by. I didn't know I could cry, she says. If you'll
    only look at me, he says.
Excuse me, can I look at your baby? I don't know, the
    mother spits, Can you?
It is clear that she has never been made love to. The girl
    stares into the baby's eyes.
There is a miniature gas station in each pupil. She turns
    around, and sees the real deal
behind her. I have to go. If she steps closer, something will catch.
Say it, the baby calls after her, say it now. She is walking, startled
by her own power. The baby is screaming. The mother is
    shoving something pink
into his slit of a mouth. It is not enough, this body. She can
    barely breathe. It is winter.
She arrives at the shore of her death with the sudden knowledge
that if she says it, everyone will have to see her. The gas clerk
flaccidly filling up a tank looks up. Their eyes meet, and then,
like brushing away a fly, he looks away. It, she begins.
He glances up to find petals of blood falling from her
    wrist. He is waiting,
the nozzle in his hand singing gasoline. It is not
a fist.

EXCUSE ME, I LOST MY COMPASS, CAN I BORROW YOURS

How do lesbians have sex? My friend Samantha and I are
   driving back
from the airport, having a deep one-on-one. Hell if I know, I say.
Samantha is straight with a boyfriend and bisexual hopes
and I've been a lesbian for at least all my life so I figure
one of us should know. When neither of us does,
it is a bit of a splinter in the conversation. She doesn't make
any uninformed guesses and I don't talk about friction.
I always dove into women without wondering
what my dive looked like and now here was Samantha
asking, What kind is that? I'll ask my mother, is all I can
   think to say.
When I go home for winter break that is just what I do.
Mom is eating Kashi like a middle-aged lesbian when I ask her.
I've never had sex with a woman, she answers. Ask your father.
When I approach him he is on the computer. Let's look
it up on the internet, he says. "Her First Time" by Reba Romaine
pops up in the search. Like the lettuce, I say. Lettuce, he says,
engrossed in what he's reading. Hey! I say—feeling like
   he's winning.
We are both surprised to learn that the first rule to lesbian sex is
masturbation. Before you can even think about turning
someone else on, it is good to know what excites you.
That doesn't even involve another woman, I say.
If I touch myself is that lesbian sex? He raises his eyebrows

like a dog might if he had eyebrows. I get distracted for a moment,
imagining this. Listen to this, he says: As you touch yourself
and find the places that feel good, you'll know where to touch her.
But her vagina isn't my vagina. And why hasn't Reba
even said the word vagina yet? Rule number two: Go sober.
You want to remember your first lesbian sex. I know I do,
        my father says,
copying and pasting. These don't seem specific to lesbians! I shout,
and in the next room, my sister shouts back What? And I
        say Come here, Abby.
And she says, What? And I say, Oh my god forget it, and
        she says, What?
Rule number three: Fantasize. It all begins with fantasy.
        Does she throw you down
on the bed and have her way with you? Or do you go
        skinny dipping in
your backyard pool? Have you ever considered this? my
        father asks.
I never considered, I always just did, I say. Hmm, he says,
        that may be your first problem
right there. By rule number ten, Reba still hasn't said
        vagina. She tells my father and I
not to use sex toys when having our first lesbian sex. That
        the first time should be
simple flesh-on-flesh love. She tells us not to go straight
        for the crotch.
To undress her slowly. To kiss her elbows. To caress her belly
and inner thighs. To kiss behind her knees. To slowly suck
        her fingers.

She ends with telling us to lie naked on top of our lesbian
    lover. Then what? I ask him.
He reads aloud the last step: Enjoy. At the bottom of the webpage,
Reba lists seventeen links, including: How to Use a Dildo,
Lesbian Anal Sex, and How to Keep Love Fresh and New.
Great, I say to my father, I have nothing to bring back to
    Samantha.
Is that your new lesbian lover? my father asks. Maybe she knows
how to have lesbian sex, he says. Abby shouts something
    incoherent
from the next room. Go ask your sister, my father says,
    clicking a link.
I walk up to my sister with my hands on my hips, which
    makes me feel matronly,
and ask. Just ask the next woman you have lesbian sex
    with, says Abby.
When I get back I report to Samantha what Abby said and
    to my surprise
Samantha says, Let's find out. I begin by undressing her slowly.
I avoid the crotch. I kiss her elbows. I caress her belly
and inner thighs. I even kiss her behind the knees, which
    feels really gay.
Then, it is a blur—I am diving and she is water and I am water
and she is diving and breath is tangled with breath and for
    one flash
of a second we are above water. We are lying next to each
    other in the dark
when Samantha asks me if she is a lesbian now. I mean, I say,
You're a woman and I'm a woman. Right, she says, calculating
something in her head. What are you thinking, I ask.

I don't feel like a lesbian, she says. I don't either. And then
   I don't know
what else to say so I say, Your skin tastes like applebutter.

ANDREA GIBSON

THANK GOODNESS
(for Buddy Wakefield)

At the end of your ten day meditation retreat
you got in your car
drove thirty peaceful feet
and ran over a bird,
splayed its holy guts on the pavement
like God finger-painting "F U"
across that deep breath you were holding
the way your mother held her first born.
You
thank goodness
were torn from the Bible
the day before they burned it
for the verse about dancing to tambourines.

Once you saw the blood of Christ
on a knife carving redwood trees into church pews.
Now every Sunday morning you hear glaciers melting
and you cry easy as a one night stand
never ever is
when you see the feathers in your rear-view mirror
scattering like prayers
searching for a safe place to land.

Hold me to my word
when I tell you I will leave today,

catch a bus ticket west
just to stand in the center of your highway
blocking traffic 'til every feather's answered.
I've seen too many prayers caught in the grills of 18 wheelers
and folks like us
got shoulder blades that rust in the rain,
but they're still g sharp
whenever our spinal chords are tuned
to the key of redemption.

So go ahead world
pick us
to make things better.

We've been building a bridge
through the center of this song
since Mother Theresa replaced the walls of her church
with the weeping cries of Calcutta's orphaned ghettos.
You wanna know what the right wing never got?
We never question the existence of God.

What we question is his bulldozer
turning Palestine into a gas chamber.
What we question is the manger in Macy's
and the sweatshops our children call the North Pole.
What we question are the sixty swollen lashes
on the back of a girl found guilty of the crime
of allowing herself to be brutally raped.
What we question is the idea of a heaven having gates.
Silly.

Have you never stood on the end of pier
watching the moon live up to her name?
Have you never looked in the eyes of a thief
and seen his children's hungry bellies?

Some days my heart beats so fast
my ribcage sounds like a frickin' railroad track
and my breath is a train I just   can't   catch.
So when my friends go filling their lungs with YES,
when they're peeling off their armor
and falling like snowflakes on your holy tongue, God
collects the feathers.

We are thick skin
covering nothing but wishbones.
Break in—
You'll find notebooks full of jaw lines
we wrote to religion's clenched fist.
Yeah—we bruise easy,
but the sound of our bouncing back
is a grand canyon full of choir claps
and our five pointed stars
have always been open to the answer—
whatever it is.

I know David argued with the chisel.
I know he said, *Make me softer.*
When those tourists come looking for a hero
I want the rain to puddle in my pours.

Build me holy like that.
Build me a kite flown out a bedroom window at midnight
the day freedom set its curfew to 9:11.
My heaven is a snow globe.
The blizzard will always be worth the touch of a hand
shaking me awake
like a boy taking deep breaths
all the way down to the dents in his shins
like he's building a telephone from a string and two tin
     cans.
He knows God's number by heart.
He knows it isn't listed in any book.

Look me in the bull's eye,
in the laws I broke
and the promises I didn't,
in the batteries I found when the lights went out
and the prayers I found when the brakes did too.
I got this moment
and no idea when it will end.
But every second of this life is scripture
and to know that
trust me
we don't need to be born

again.

ASHES

(for all those in the GLBTQ community killed in the name of God)

The night I was torn from the pages of their Bible
and burned alive
my ashes came down like snow
and a girl who had never seen my face
saw me falling from the sky
and laid down on her back
to make an angel in the powder of my bones.

From heaven I watched her,
though my eyes were still flame,
and my ribs were still blue.
They didn't win, I whispered, as her arms built my wings.
They didn't win.
Look at that moon.
It is a pebble in my hand.
Tonight I could skip it across that fog drunk sea
til their lashes accordion in the light
and all they know of hate
is that it couldn't beat the love out of me. . . .

that when they dropped me to the grave
I fell like a bucket into a well
and came up full
carving my lover's name
into the skin of weeping willow

that had spent its entire life laughing at the rain.

Hold me like a lantern.
Staircase my spine.
When they bring their children to my funeral
to scream "FAGGOT" at my dust
tell them I was born into their casket
but I wouldn't pull the splinters from my heart
any more than Christ would have pulled the thorns
from his crimson head.

They can come a thousand times
with their burning match and their gasoline,
with their hungry laws
and their empty mouths full of prayers to that God
who greeted me at his gates with his throat full of trumpets
and his tears full of shame
as his trembling palms collected the cinder of his children's crime.

I know what holy is.
I know the soul is shaped like a bowl.
I know the lies we try to fill it with,
and we spill too often the orchards inside.

But my lover's shoes were laced with guitar stings
and when I walked beside
there was a silo in my chest.
There was a field full of sun.
There was a river full of gold that we left
to pick our sweethearts from trees

that kept uprooting tombstones
so the names of the dead could crumble into poems.

Write me down like this:
Say my ashes never made the news.
Say the jury was full of shotguns.
Then say the snow that is falling on the tip of your tongue
will refuse to melt away.
Say this to the kids hiding their beat beats from their fathers'
     fists.
I planted the garden of my kiss.
I opened the night with my teeth.
I loved so hard that when you press your ear to the track,
the train they hear coming will still be my chest,
a rumbling harpoon—
a love they can bury.

Look at that moon—I am a pebble in her hand,
a harmonica held to the mouth of the river
where nothing ever
burns.

EVERY MONTH

Every month
when I get my period
I breathe a sigh of relief
and thank God I'm not pregnant
cause you never know
when Jesus is coming back
and you never know who God's gonna choose
to be the next Virgin Mary
and can you imagine anything more scary
than staring down between your legs
and seeing the little glowing head of Baby Jesus?
Holy Lord, no thank you!!

I mean, what kind of bumper sticker would you get?
Your son's an honor student?
Yeah well—*My son* walks on water and cures lepers, suckers!!

Think of the pressure.

Personally I'd prefer to give birth to Lucifer,
a fixer-upper,
the kind of kid who would sit at the last supper
and complain that Judas got more mashed potatoes
cause God knows
the holy have done more damage to this world
than the devil ever could.

CRAB APPLE PIRATES

(Calais, ME)

We were chubby-faced school kids,
snicker bar wind-piped, crab apple pirates,
backward baseball-capped knee scraped snow angels,
dukes of hazard dreamers, bumper car bodied salamander catchers,
Michael Jordan believers.

I couldn't fly, but my hang time was three minutes
and ten seconds.

Smart kids were stupid.
Books were trees cut down.
I was a tomboy in love with Malcolm Cushion.
He had a birthmark in the shape of Canada on his left cheek.
The teachers didn't trust him.
His mother was the accidental broken tooth in a bar fight.

I had one black friend.
Her name was Erica.
She had a jackknife.
She carved a gash into the center of her palm, another into mine.
We pressed our hands together and she asked
if I thought it would turn her blood white.
I couldn't read her fear or hope.
I thought history was over.
I cried during the national anthem.

Once I found a butterfly's wing on the sidewalk.
I wanted to keep it but I didn't.
I knew there were things I should never find beautiful.
Like death.
And girls.

On Saturdays I walked around town with a wheelbarrow
collecting aluminum cans.
On Sundays my father paid a penny
for every cigarette butt I'd pick up in the driveway.
I was picking up cigarette butts
when Tommy Chambers punched my tooth out.
I spit on his bike seat and beat the crap out of his older brother.

I started writing songs.
Recorded them on my ghetto blaster
and mailed the tapes to the local radio station
but they never played them
because they never had good taste.

My mother did.
She was a secretary.
Her fingernails were red
and she loved my father,
who after the war became a mailman
so when I was a baby she would carry me to the post office
and weigh me on the postal scales.

Once, years later, I got lost in the mail.
The next day I came home from college and
corrected my father's grammar.

When I was ten my mother had another daughter.
I had heard babies sometimes die in their sleep
so at night when my parents went to bed
I'd put on my Karate Kid kimono
and I'd sneak into her room to guard her heartbeat.

The heartbeat thieves didn't find her for fifteen years.

At eleven I discovered beer.
At fourteen I accepted Jesus Christ as my personal Lord
    and Savior.
At nineteen I nailed my palm to Amanda Bucker's vagina,
actually drooled on her breasts,
and said *yes* so loud God couldn't disagree.

But my family did.
So I lost them for a while, and in that while
my uncle Barry lost his fingers to the paper mill.
My uncle Peter lost his liver to Vietnam.
My mother lost her legs to God's will.

In her will I inherit everything:
the seventeen photographs we didn't lose in the fire,
all of them with charcoaled edges.
My mother holds them to her chest and tells
me she can still smell the smoke.

I tell her I will guard them well,
my father's freckled shoulders,
my sister's brown, brown eyes,
my mother's patient hands buckling my tiny blue suspenders,
that one December when we built a bonfire in the middle
of the frozen lake
and I skated around the flames
with my snowsuit's frozen zipper sticking to
my tongue.

My father said, *smile for the camera*.
I can still remember the flash.
And that enormous fire.
With the ice beneath it.
That didn't even crack.

MIKE MCGEE

THE END

If I should die today
I hope I've done all the laughing
I can let out of this body
I hope it was contagious
I hope it was heard and appreciated

I hope a great many people remember
the fact that I was here
Not remembered like
Shakespeare or Mussolini
Remembered more along the lines of
a much simpler person
Like Gandhi...Albert Gandhi
who lived down the street from me and
loved food and women as if
they were oxygen and humor

Because there is no Albert Gandhi
that I know of
I made him up and
that's funny to me

If I die today
I want the world to be able
to go on without me
Even though I know
it will be incredibly hard

If I die today
I should be cremated
or properly taxidermied
I imagine I'd make one fabulous lawn gnome
It really doesn't matter what is done with my remains
but please...do not auction off my genitalia

If I should die today
I hope those who knew me well
will tell the world that I was
rarely ever serious
That inciting laughter was always
my primary goal
That by experiencing
someone else's joy
I lived it as well

When ordering my tombstone
please have the date of my death
span three or four days
    I want people to think of it
    as a big event they may have missed out on

    McGee-A-palooza

If I die today
I want everyone
I've loved and liked
to know that I've
appreciated them very much

You've made this world
a hell of a lot more tolerable
    I hope my life was worth your time
    as yours was worth every second of mine

Should I die today
make note that I
am not ready for it
But I've accomplished
centuries in my decades and
for that I am grateful

So please enjoy tomorrow for me

If you can hear this
you're invited to my funeral
especially if you promise to
shut the fuck up every
once in a while and just listen
    to keep fighting the good fight
    to always do what is right
        and before you go
        tell the sun I said hello and
            kiss the moon goodnight

GEEZ, US!

I was hanging out with Jesus the other day
drinking grape soda on His balcony
We watched the sun go down beyond Los Angeles
I had hoped for wine
He said I should have brought some
We talked a lot
I asked Him what it was like to die
He said it was His favorite of all His Dad's art projects

> *Death is so quick compared to life*
> *because it is that awesome*

I asked Jesus what He liked about today and
it took Him too long to respond
I dozed off and dreamed of four men on Shetland ponies
riding around, breaking windows
        They were the Four Midgets of the Apocalypse
        They burned down miniature golf courses
        and stabbed people below the waist

Jesus woke me up and
presented me with an omelet
which was delicious
As any evening breakfast would be
when made by the Son of God

I told Him that He seemed like the cool older brother I
never had
He thought that was cool and asked me to stop
masturbating so much

I told Him that every day I feel a certain sense of
unexplainable loneliness
He said it was because I spend too much time alone
I pondered that for a moment while He offered me hash
browns

His apartment was decorated with film posters from
    movies
that told His story in some way
Last Temptation of Christ
Jesus Christ Superstar
and *Repo Man*

One of the posters was signed by Willem Dafoe
He spoke well of Willem Dafoe
but Jesus doesn't own a DVD player

Over time
I got the feeling that the human part of Him wants to be
    forgotten
but the heavenly side is anxious to introduce everyone to
His Dad

I asked Him why He moved to L.A.

He said it was the hidden beauty
    That having to search for the good
    meant that when it was found
    it had to be authentic
He also pointed out that L.A. is one of the few places
a man dressed like Him can still go unnoticed in public

We watched Mexican television
He interpreted all of the game shows and soap operas
It stayed warm well into the night
so I slept on the balcony
while Jesus wandered the streets
looking for lost souls

In the morning
He woke me to another omelet
this time wrapped in a big flour tortilla
I wasn't hungry so He wrapped it and put it in a bag

Then He asked me to shave His head
I felt uncomfortable
He said it was okay
and that His strength came from somewhere else
He just wanted to fit in with the rest of us

I shaved His head
and waddled home

Later that afternoon
I noticed one of His hairs stuck to my collar

If I had a girlfriend and she found it before me
she might wonder who it came from
    but I don't
    and she can't
    and so she won't

I pulled out the breakfast burrito
and birthed it from its aluminum foil
I noticed a face burned into the tortilla
A surprising miracle for me to enjoy
He knew I wouldn't share it with anyone else

It made me wonder how often Jesus
promoted Himself with food items
For every one hundred new Starbucks
that opens around the world
a statue of Him cries chocolate milk

I ate my holy burrito neck first
and smiled
once I realized
that it was actually the face of Willem Dafoe

IN SEARCH OF MIDNIGHT

Somewhere in the cold midnight of Idaho
two women prepare to leave town together.
They're tired of drawing public attention to
the way they hold each other's hands.

    (Couples in Idaho do hold hands, they just don't
    usually look like two women.)

So they hit the road for California
where people still segregate themselves from each other
and every city's East Side is feared by sub-urbanites
because the local news anchor hates the East Side
so he reminds us
every night on the nightly news
just how dangerous it is with
all of its minorities and crime.

He prefers downtown at midnight
where he can afford to be a teenager again
and maybe even on top of one.

Somewhere on the East Side of Vancouver, British
    Columbia
a fourteen-year-old woman
hops on a bus to get to Hastings Street, downtown
where her body is worth a little bit more.

She wonders if any girl has ever
taken their pimp to the school prom and
watches out for all the hookers who are younger than her.
Dead mothers cannot question a child who sleeps through
the afternoon.

When she has enough money
she'll catch a bus to Montreal or Toronto
and dance for the rest of her life
but currently
it is midnight
and she has rent to make.

At midnight in Hollywood, there are waiters and
waitresses practicing their Academy Award acceptance
speeches while serving you chicken wings and hash
browns.

At midnight in Denver, there are poets who heat up their
dinners on radiators and wash their clothes by hand
cause quarters are saved for buses and homeless people.

At midnight in San Antonio, a man holds a party because
the body warmth will heat up his house just long
enough for him to get a few hours of sleep before
teaching his elementary school class in the morning.

At midnight in Portland, a college student sleeps in
someone else's bed every night just so she can continue
her education.

At midnight in Seattle, a man hears a poem that might
keep him alive for one more day.

At midnight in San Diego, an illegal immigrant puts
American cash in an envelope to be mailed back to his
family in Mexico, while eating his first Big Mac on his
late-night lunch break.

At midnight in Oklahoma City, a young girl gets drunk
for the first time and realizes it is the best thing to do
because it is the only thing to do.

At midnight in Chicago, a man sits in jail, for the first time
in his life, for a crime he did not commit. He knows
nobody will believe him because he knows all too well
the color of his own skin. He marvels at how far we've
come.

At midnight in some of the worst parts of Detroit, a
woman prays to her God for the first time in years
because of something she heard on the news.

She really wants tomorrow to be a better day.

At midnight in San José, a fat man puts more food into his
mouth to try to feel better about the world or forget it
all together.

At midnight throughout the rest of the world, people are
exactly who they should be.

They are you.

You are quite possibly someone you'll never share with
    anyone else.

You're the ones who could leave hot food
at the feet of sleeping homeless people
then worry about your next meal when no one is looking.
You're the one who may never function at noon
the one who everyone will believe
left the planet just a little too soon.

You might not have tongues
    but you have so much to say.

I know, I've heard you.

You are doing what it takes
    to stay sane and alive.
You are not wearing the finest clothes.
You are online and searching.
You are making free calls on phones you cannot afford.
You are reaching out to yourself
in an attempt to find perfection,

    whether it is within yourself or in someone else.

Somewhere out there
it must exist.
It must be possible to achieve

what we all want
because if it isn't
then midnight comes to us for no reason.
We start over every day for no reason.
There must be something perfect in this world
and I believe it comes to us all
at midnight.

THE SMILE

I'm sitting in the break room at work. Just outside the door is a window to the street. Anybody who walks by said window can see me in said break room.

As I ate my toasted Asiago bagel with cream cheese I lamented the fact that I had to return to work. Outside of the break room were grumpy-ass customers just waiting to yell at me and my nametag.

I continued eating when this woman walked by the window, made eye contact with me and smiled. Not a "what're you looking at" type of smile, more like: "Hey there sad eyes, take this smile from my lips. Let not this day bring you darkness, but a new light and harmony. Let thy peace be done."

It was a "Shine on you crazy diamond," kind of smile

I was awestruck by her power; she went by at the speed of modern humanity. It would have been easy to miss her noble gift as she passed me by. Being a stranger, I assumed she could only smile at chubby white men with bagel crumbs in their goatees. It is possible, however, that when our eyes met…she farted.

But that singular smile was salvation from a seemingly sucky day. Like a virus, she passed to me this simple contagion of contortion.

My face was paralyzed into a position of positivity—a smile so solid you'd swear I lost my virginity in the break room twice to Milla Jovovich wearing nothing but Scotch tape. This was beyond sexual bliss, this was me being giddy on a Monday at work thanks to a stranger on the street. She compelled me to pass on a smile doubly-wide to everyone who came before me. I left with my co-workers smiling like they'd just won a year supply of cake, milk, and weed. There I was, this giddy, pear-shaped genius, smiling so hardcore my gums were bleeding. My mission of mouth mechanics had me making mad men merry, while working wildly to wow women to wonder, "Why the fuck is he so happy?" and "How do men that chubby get so damn cute?"

I'll tell you how . . . Smiling is sexy, and I smile all the time. I am cute because I still believe smiling is the first step we can take toward helping out one person at a time. Even if I didn't have teeth, I'd still smile, because teeth are an unimportant aesthetic in the diplomacy of smiling. It's almost better than eating a free buffet dinner with a stripper at a casino where you just won three hundred bucks on a silver dollar you found in the gutter. Almost.

Abraham Lincoln didn't smile and look what happened to him

Smiles are the last proof and truth that we are beautiful, that we can do more than we believe ourselves capable. A complete stranger smiled at me, and although my life didn't attain perfection, it did get a little better.

It's as if she said, "Baby, I know how you feel, and we'll get through this." Her smile carried me throughout my day and later that afternoon I stepped into a coffee shop where I usually buy orange juice, but instead I asked the girl behind the counter if she would have dinner with me sometime. She said and nodded yes, punctuating it with a smile. It caused a revelation to smile across my brain as I realized I had never asked a woman out before, and that made me smile.

ANIS MOJGANI

CLOSER

come closer.
come into this. come closer.
you are quite the beauty. if no one has ever told you that
before know that now. you are quite the beauty. there is joy
in how your mouth dances with your teeth. your mouth is
a sign of how sacred your life truly is. come into this. true
of heart come into this. you are true of heart. come closer.
come closer. know that whatever God prays to He asked
it to help Him make something of worth. He woke from
His dreams scraped the soil form the spaces inside Himself
made you and was happy. you make the Lord happy.
come into this.
come closer.

know that something softer than us but just as holy
planted the pieces of Himself into our feet that we might
one day find our way back to Him. you are almost home.
come closer come into this. there are birds beating their
wings beneath your breastplate gentle sparrows aching to
sing come aching hearts come soldiers of joy doormen of
truth come true of heart come into this.
my heart was too big for my body so I let it go and most
days this world has thinned me to where I am just another
cloud forgetting another flock of swans but believe me
when I tell you my soul has squeezed into narrow spaces.
place your hand beneath your head when you sleep tonight

and you may find it there making beauty as we sleep as
we dream as we turn over when I turn over in the ground
may the ghosts that I have asked answers of do the turning
kneading me into crumbs of light and into this thing love
thing called life. come into it!

come you wooden museums
you gentle tigers
negro farces in two broken scenes.
come rusting giants!
I see teacups in your smiles upside down glowing. your
hands are like my heart. on some days how it trembles.
let us hold them together. I am like you. I too at times am
filled with fear. but like a hallway must find the strength to
walk through it. walk through this with me. walk through
this with me. through this church birthed of blood and
muscle where every move our arms take every breath we
swallow is worship.
bend with me. there are bones in our throats. if we choke it
is only on songs.

LOVE IS NOT A SCIENCE

the bedroom is a morgue
the bed a slot car race
memories are a rock thrown through the window of an
    empty house
love is a shirt you still wear that has already stopped fitting
flowers all have names
the same names
the moon is a son of a bitch
the sun a mean mean star
the stars are tombstones
the constellations a graveyard
the flowers reach past their bones
to lay themselves across the feet of dead animals
the dead animal is a quiet sadness
a quiet cross made over the chest
a prayer is a quiet kiss
given to the solar system
the flowers all have the same names
a rooftop is a telephone to heaven
a telephone call has the sound of dirt filling the grave back up
a conversation is a knife fight
the heart a flat tire
the northwest was a lighthouse
a joyous shout
now a stain
portland a deep hole I am trying to dig my way out of

the city of eugene is a conman who stole my shovel
ireland is a theft
los angeles a lie
new orleans
is a sad sad porch
it carries the baskets of little girls' slanted truths
the past is littered with no trespassing signs
writing poetry is drinking from a broken bottle
memories are a broken vase whose shape everyone
      remembers differently
I remember it having flowers
a box is for holding its petals
flowers all have one name
goodbye is a pocketknife that doesn't close properly
goodnight is an echo
sleep sweetly an emptied rabbit hutch
the blanket replaces people
a teacup is too small a replacement
people replace a lover
sleep is a battlefield
God takes naps
He dreams of the people who have left Him behind
animals are saints
learning to touch them brings one closer to that which
      was holy
the unicorn is not a lie the unicorn is real
I've seen it
its skin is blue not white
dance is a magic trick she rarely showed me
all I ever wanted was to see up her sleeves

the wrist is a lifeboat
the memory is death dressed in sanctuary
the small town of milwaukie is a garden
the flowers there all grow in the direction of her mother's house
they all speak one name
my tears move their mouths when they speak it
her hand holding mine is a war I am afraid of losing
hope is a blindfold
thighs are a safehouse
the embrace is bathwater
the backbone a song
the body is Buddha singing it
the ear Krishna eating an apple behind it
the neck a monastery
a kiss the rosary
the mouth an orchard
her teeth sweet cherries
the words she says when sleeping are church
I would follow them over any mountain
her voice is a big smile of a man who knows the way to go
her voice is a big man I would follow over any mountain
her voice is a mitten
her voice is too far away
it is made up of air and vibrations
I do not know how to put my hands inside of that
her eyes are the blue hairs of a horned horse running
my eye lids are closet doors
my eyes skeletons searching for hangars to hang
    themselves off of
every day I put on this coat of knives

just try and hold me
just try and hold me
just try
to hold me

PARADE DAY

confetti and graffiti give me the same feeling
like something won or someone came home from far far away
there are days when I am surprised the streets are not run
    rampant with both
that there is not kissing in the streets
that there is not the rock song everlasting of fireworks explosion
that the streets are not overflowing
with slow-driving convertible parades
and beautiful queens
waving at us
there are some hours where I am surprised
that there is no parade scheduled
simply because we all woke up and did it—
we were human!
today!
we were human!
yesterday! we were the same thing
and tomorrow—
again!
filled with blue mountain lust and skyscraper
we are skyscrapers
we are whatever is bigger than skyscrapers
broken balls of gas and matter that have traveled far
from whatever corner spat them out
in the contraction and expansion of space
that is the same pulse of the forest

sections of this universe that moved through space
until it found something soft to move through
bits of paper broken and torn
from larger sheets
curved and curling in the wind
sign your name across my back
it is not the concrete poured into the foundation
that makes the buildings able to stand up every day
but rather the words burned across their faces and feet
that some stranger loved them or loved themselves enough
    to do that
sign your name across my back
it ain't the cinder in the timber
but the initials carved that break the trunk open
the tree flaunting its body
saying
look at me
look at what I got
somebody loved something hard enough to use a knife
look at what I got

STARTING

i am in blue shorts and her
in orange dress
walking down the heat of austin
both our eyes closed
trying to see how far we can walk with them like that
blind except for our hands in each other's
the smell of a magnolia in our memory from the block before
with the street ravining next to my left foot
speeding with cars
and our eyes still clenched closed tight as a seed
we make it halfway down the block
all the way to the bus stop

MINDY NETTIFEE

THE CONNECTION BETWEEN GOD AND NATURE BEATS ME OVER THE HEAD WITH ITS EARTHY MALLET

I woke up an atheist today
and it is definitely connected
to the "Chakra Magic Lunar Calendar"
pinned by my kitchen window,
its daylights punched out with black x's
marking the nights I've gone without stars.

The Long Beach sunsets are trying to help.
They are massaging my temples with their melted romance,
calming me down with the blood pressure medication
of their mellow collisions with the sky.

Thanks.

But I could really use some starlight.
The unadulterated kind.
The canopy of brash burning asterisks
illuminating the vast deep.
My back crashing its shares of gravity to the earth.
My entire field of vision a complex astronomy,
the universe glittering its jewelry,
my mouth hung open like a starving fish—
hooked—
breathing shallow in the cold damp midnight.

This is day 3,042 of my inner struggle with city life.

I am staring dreamily out the kitchen window,
watching sunlight smelt and sweat in the steam from a cup of tea.
I am picturing myself *ranching*, if that's even a verb.
Later I will pause in the hallway of my apartment,
having just bruised my hip on broken bookshelves,
and fantasize about the sexy promises of open space,
like high school girls in farmhouses must fantasize
about being crushed in the wasted pulsing crowds at rock concerts.

This distance from the land:
it's a sacrifice you make, however temporarily,
to live huddled with the other artists and smart alecks,
to go *months* without being called a liberal hippie
by someone who says it like it's a cancer in his mouth.

It's a choice that makes itself for me
every time I am rescued by the warm clotted glow of art galleries,
by the imitation of Django Reinhardt that is really not that bad,
strumming rakishly out of the mood lit punk bar,
or the old David Bowie juke-boxing the punchy patrons
at the cheaper bar down the street.

In the absence of starlight
you start looking for the shine in everything:
the sparkle of fresh-paved asphalt.
The glinting litter of crinkled candy wrappers.
The gold fillings in a smile so big you could live in it.
With no forest of trees for comparison,
the smallest signs of life are magic.

God refuses to be outdone by the metropolis.

When you are most homesick, inexplicably,
for some place you've never even lived,
an unexpected ocean breeze salts the heavy air,
stirring everything.

It says: your happiness will return to you
like the prodigal son,
having spent your inheritance of expectations extravagantly,
but ready now to do the work of joy.
Have faith.

The signs of life gather themselves in any darkness.
It's a rebirth, a rebuilding, of what was never really destroyed.
In what is its own kind of starlight,
a thousand bright minds flicker on,
our imaginations like flashlights,
searching for a path,
blinking in the dark.

WHAT COMES AFTER

All night I had been drinking the edges of your face away
with an old friend whose cola eyes could spark wet matchsticks
and who still laughed with her entire body,
even though she had just discovered her husband neck-deep in
the stiff ruffled panties of her 22-year-old nanny.

We were both broken and stinging
in that way that trust with its stuck blade
will turn and cut you open without your permission.

So we drank until we were righteous and gorgeous again.
We drank until we spilled guts
like we were subsidized gut factories.
We drank until our metaphors got fat and ridiculous
and toppled over themselves,
and we could no longer agree
whether the war on women had had its Hiroshima

or whether the "test" or the "tost" in "testosterone"
turned men into weapons.
I got so belligerent on this point
that the goth girl bartender at the punk bar
had to ask *me* to "settle down."
   Screw you, Bettie Whatever!
   Here's my number.

Call me when you're finished fashioning chopsticks from
eyebrows.
Call me when you're finished sewing Dear John letters to
your bed sheets.
Call me when your angst has expanded to outer space,
  and you're piloting your hopelessmobile to hell,
at which point I fell off the barstool.

Our money having lost its cashiness at that particular bar
we sat on the roof of her parked car
scheming for more booze and watching
the 2 a.m. women's liberation parade
stumble past us in miniskirts and purple lingerie,
purposefully torn tee-shirts with girly power slogans,

all clambering after lanky blonde boys bruised from bar fights—
the kind of cheap display of irony from all of us
that makes you sympathize with burqas,
or want to burn your Victoria's Secret bra
on the doorstep of the local strip joint,
even if you *loved* that bra,
even if you loved bras in general,
which is precisely what would happen later
after we'd found and finished another bottle of rum.

Hey, she asked, in a voice reserved for lovers high on worship,
you want to see my scar? and pulled the waist of her jeans down
to show me where her daughter had been cut out of her.
I traced the smooth crescent of raised skin with my fingers
    reverently.

She began humming a tune I had never heard before.
It sounded like a love song to mangoes and butcher knives.
Like a hymn for daughters and rebels and killer wives.

I don't know how we made it home.

When we found my doorstep,
we were laughing so hard the quiet night frowned.
We could barely stand,
so we rested our foreheads together in praise of gravity.
I swear I could feel the dawning of something—
what comes after bitterness,
low in the stomach like sick bees.
I could feel the soft thing that replaces it,
that makes a body ask for forgiveness
by turning slowly to the song.

TO THE BEST THING THAT EVER HAPPENED TO ME

I am writing you from an eight-foot snow drift
somewhere south of somewhere.

I would call, but I lost my cell phone two days ago
at the ice rink pity party that was really just me,
a frozen lake, some cheap Russian vodka, and
a depressed polar bear. (Those guys are dark.)

I still have six waterproof matches
and what Vogue Magazine assures me
is twenty extra pounds of body fat.
No, I am not proud of myself.
No, I am not "done with my obsession with Survivalism."

But I am sorry; I am sorry we fought.

You were right when you said writing poetry is not a real skill
applicable post-apocalypse, and I said but who will tell the
    good stories,
and you said guys who can fish with their bare hands.

It turns out that's really hard.
Trout are ticklish,
and my hands do not have to do what I tell them to,
some sort of freezing cold water clause.

I have nothing but the time and space I've been pining for now,
and I am using this opportunity to try and remember
why I thought this was a good idea.

I think it had something to do with escape,
which has permanent offices in the romance division of my brain
and ground troops in my solar plexus.

The flight instinct comes on quicksand,
muscles out all rational thought,
starts Morse coding my limbic system with
complex dots and dashes for strange verbs that mean,
roughly translated: "joyous chewing your leash off,"
and "fire without readiness or aim."

It always feels so right to go,
like it's the only story my body knows by heart:
the creation myth of Alaskan shorebirds,
the bedtime story highways whisper to dirt roads,
the real reason horses sometimes obey.
You really wanted to marry me, didn't you?

My eyelashes are soaked now.
I'm beginning to think I will never see you again,
that I will never see anything again
but the twenty yards or so of visibility
in stark panorama around my broken sled.
I feel like an idiot, but I'm not scared.
You'd think I would be scared.

These are the soft frozen fields tundra vacations too,
the great white quiet.
No one to distrust.
I deserve this.
You would be amazed how much light there is.
The stars stay out all night.
Each snowflake is a mirror.

AFTER THE FUNERAL

I can't tell if I'm hungry or just empty.

The floorboards won't creak.

There's no bottle of stolen scotch on the mantle.
The Elmore James records won't ache like they used to.
There's no spirit of Charles Bukowski stenching up the place,
no cats in the alleyway, mawing.

There should be.

There's no cinema in this.

I miss cigarettes.
It's just me and my ugliness now.
The two-day-old wine will have to do.

Someday, I want to erect a museum to the world's worst ministers,
the ones who downward spiral drone,
who get increasingly boring the closer they get to their point.
We'll line up stuttering seven-year-olds still learning to read
in the main exhibit hall. We'll dress them in itchy vestments
and have them recite the most moving passages of the Bible aloud.

I'll name the audience participation cringe-o-meter after you.

The minister that performed your funeral told me you are
    with Jesus now.
That if I don't find Jesus, wherever he is hiding, I'll never
    see you again.
I *know* I'll never see you again.
It's not killing me. It's just digging slow graves in my heart.
I hate when ministers mix their anthropomorphic metaphors,
when they confuse mourning with porousness.

This wine tastes like battery acid, with strong berry notes,
and a fuck-you finish.
Its sour bitchiness is so familiar it's like drinking a mirror.

Wow. And I'm not even drunk yet.
My mother is probably right.
I shouldn't be alone.
I don't know if I believe in ghosts,
but I can picture them, so what's the difference?

I'm picturing you now, some gray cloud of you,
pulled everywhere that remembering creates anchors.
You're counting crocodile tears,
able to see clearly now, finally,
but still collecting evidence to prove it,
the schizophrenia having shaped you even after death.

You're watching us, memorizing the details of our grief—
your wife's skeletal figure, bent over the toilet.
Your father staring daggers at the walls.
Your mother digging a fat finger in the prescription bottle.

You want to wrap each detail in paper.
You want to keep it, but you don't know how.
You grow more desperate as we grow less desperate.
You try to memorize faster, pulling at our sadness like a
    kite on its string,
even as what's left of your mind starts to dissipate,

even as your soul form evaporates,
at first softly, then violently,
like white hair chopping in the wind.

SHAPPY SEASHOLTZ

I'M LOVING IT

Yes, I know YOU never eat there.
Yes, I know it's not good for you.
Yes, I know they are an eyesore in every city and
    highway exit.
Yes, I saw *Super Size Me* and guess what?

It made me crave two all-beef patties, special
sauce, lettuce, cheese, pickles, onions on a sesame seed
bun!

That's right, my friends, I will climb to the top of
Hamburger Hill and scream to the heavenly heavens...

I LOVE McDONALD'S!!!

I love the milkshakes that have no dairy in them
whatsoever!

I love the salty pressed potato product they call
french fries!

I love the orange drink that has tasted the same since
the 1970's.

I love how no matter where I go, how far I travel, the
food always tastes the same.

How is that POSSIBLE?!?
It is truly a magical miracle of food engineering!

I love the Dollar Menu (even though everything in
Manhattan is $1.29).

I love how they thought that a SCARY CLOWN was the way
to go for a CORPORATE MASCOT and that he has a huge,
purple, diabetic, milkshake-stealing best friend named
GRIMACE!

I love buying Happy Meals so I can get the cool toys
for myself!

I love how they are re-modeling all of their "dining
areas" to look like STARBUCKS so people will want to
hang out there.

I love how there is always a gaggle of senior citizens
sitting in the "dining area" drinking endless cups of
coffee.

I love the breakfast menu, and, I shit you not, if I
have to be awake before noon, there is a ninety percent chance
I will be eating a sausage biscuit with two hash
browns.

I love that feeling that when I am eating there, I am
eating with AMERICA, the whole greasy lot of them!

God bless us all!
We all eat there.
We have all eaten there.
We would miss it if they closed tomorrow.

So, up yours, Spurlock!
I'll never read *Fast Food Nation*!
You can't make me!
I deserve a break today!
So yes, I will take two apple pies for a dollar!
Thank you, Ray Kroc, for making this country three billion
hamburgers strong!

WHALE SONG FOR MY BASTARD SON

When that asshole
knocked me up
I slapped that bastard
across the face
and thanked him
for planting another worthless seed
in my bleeding field
of broken dreams

When the greedy little fetus
parted my beef curtains
and spat out on the hospital floor
the doctor kicked me in the tits
and said
"Thanks for bringing another worthless life into the world
I hope he gets murdered"

As I gathered my latest mistake
into my bruised and tattooed arms
I wondered how many packs of cigarettes he might be
    worth

I hated him

I loved him

As he grew up
I let him know how he burned me
every time he touched me
with his rusty needle fingers

Once, he brought me a broken baby bird
he found on the sidewalk
His leaky radiator eyes told me
he was afraid of death

"Don't be afraid of death,"
I whispered into the mush melon head
"Embrace it"

My son peed on the floor
as if to say
"I understand, Mommy"

When my son turned five
he brought me a necklace made of bullets
he found next to an old dead wino
who smelled like an exquisite merlot
That had been uncorked too soon

"Keep these," I whispered
"You may need them someday"

My son
my baby boy

kept the bullets in a shoebox with the word
"FREEDOM"
scrawled on the lid in crayon
next to a faded picture of his sister
who was raped then hit by a bus
I almost remember her

When my boy turned 16
he told me to go fuck myself

When my boy turned 17
he text messaged me
"Go fuck yourself"
I knew then that he meant it

When my boy turned 18
he murdered me

And yet, I'm the one
who went to prison

A prison
made of
cigarette butts
bullets
and
baleen.

ZOMBIE STAND-UP

Thank you! Thank you!
What a wonderful audience!

There am nothing more beautiful than
the sound of rotting fleshing slapping together!

That's what she said!

Me kidding, me kidding!
Me eat own penis long time ago…

Cause that's where's men's brains are!
Am me right, ladies?!

Speaking of fairer sex,
ever notice when female zombie eat brains,
she sit down, but when male zombie eat brains,
he stand up?

What am up with that?

On to current events,
remember when we stormed White House
thinking we would find brains?

Last time we did something that ironic
was when we ate George Romero's brain!

Me time almost up,
but let me know leave with this—

Me may not be the funniest zombie comic
you'll ever see—but it's un-living!

SHAPPY'S ANGELS

Sammy was a little rat-fuck punk bully.
He used to give me Indian burns during recess.
At the age of 7 he was already wearing cowboy boots,
torn Levis, and Black Sabbath t-shirts.
White trash in training under the guidance of his
older, stoner-freak brother Dennis who was 18 and
still in the 9th grade.
Dennis would cruise around the mean streets of
Kettering, Ohio, in his custom van with chicks named
Tami with an "i."
I imagine he got them baked in exchange for a hand job
at the A&W drive-in.
Soon this lifestyle would be embraced by Sammy but
that is now and this is then.
Like any healthy prepubescent lad in the
mid-seventies, I enjoyed the curious boner I'd get
from watching *Charlie's Angels*.
I grew up in a neighborhood of girls far from Sammy's
turf.
I would be called upon to play the part of Bosley,
advising the femme fatales and giving them their
orders from Charlie (a role I often find myself in
to this day!).
The mission: acquire Slush Puppies from the United
Dairy Farmers on the corner and await further orders.
As Bosley I played it cool while perusing an issue of

The Micronauts at the comic book rack when something caught my eye.

Next to the *Happy Days* cards was an unopened box of (GASP!) CHARLIE'S ANGELS TRADING CARDS!!! I bought five packs and slipped four more packs in my tube socks. I spent that night slowly unwrapping pack after pack of heavenly bodies. My hands were all sticky the next morning FROM ALL THE GUM I CHEWED! The next day at recess I was still drooling over card number 37—"Jill goes to the beach!"—when suddenly— BAM—in the knees!

POW—I'm eating dirt.

SOCK—trading cards scattered

and the wind cried . . . Sammy.

"Gimmie those fuckin' cards, pussy!"

"Leave me alone, Sammy. Please!"

"Awwww, widdle baby wants his baseball cards . . . what the fuck? *Charlie's Angels*? What are you, Seasholtz? A FAG?"

"No, Sammy . . . you are."

"What'd you say, Seasholtz? You callin' me a fag, FAG?"

Suddenly I heard a trio of heavenly voices.

"Drop the cards dirtbag! We have you surrounded! Leave Bosley alone!"

"Fuck you! *Charlie's Angels* sucks!"

And the skies split open and the girls pelted Sammy with dodgeballs.

"Ow! Quit it! I'm tellin' on you guys!"

The neighborhood girls came over and helped me up as I dusted myself off.

"Are you all right, Bosley?"

"I am. Thanks to you, Angels!"

SONYA RENEE TAYLOR

PENANCE

Messiah mother,
I waited for your second coming
pressed beneath the hips of men
whose faces never morphed into yours.
Could never cradle me like you.
Searched for salvation in their
sweat, saliva, and sweet lies,
biding time till your return.

You are finally here and broken
in all the places I need desperately to be whole.
There is an 8-year-old I lay down
to bed every night
inside my chest.
She doesn't sleep soundly
since you have started drinking.
Coughs her little girl cough every time
you pull a drag of that Newport.

It is useless telling her to rest.
She lost you once on her watch.
Knows mommas are snatched
when little girls are arrogant enough to dream.
Lately she does not blink or breathe either.

Sleep is a luxury of the ignorant.
Those who have never needed second coming

or sermon to summon their mother home.
Sleep is for those who will only lose her once
after she has saved them more times than
they are worth.

My apologies for hanging my
pitiful expectations on your back;
for wanting returned what is irretrievable.

Forgive me for this fear that clings
to my stomach with its small hands; twists in knots
when I smell the liquor on your breath
over the phone.

Forgive me for being only this;
less than steel and teeth.
A tiny pulp of child who needs
a sober mother
to mother her. . . .

Forgive me.

DREAMS FROM FATHER/ WRESTLING THE POSSIBLE

My daddy wrestled a lion and saved my life last night
My daddy is not the lion wrestling type.
Actually he is the "I look good for my age
but after twenty years in the US Navy
I got my ass a desk job!" kinda guy.
He's a Libra. Balanced.
Not prone to wild fits of frenzy
like fighting off two hundred pound felines.

My dad and I
don't talk much.
When we do it's all pleasantries and fluff.
The last word in every conversation is a trembling domino
terrified of being the one to start the collapse.
We are both so frightened that this house of cards
we have built on our laps will fall.
He and I are sort of like black ice,
we look just fine on the surface.
Every now and then I long for a collision;
for the invisible chaos under our wheels
to halt the pretense.
Some days I pray for a large gaping wound
to expose the blood.

I try not to ask my father for things
like money, or rides

or love.

That heavy-ass NO always falls on my chest.
Breaks shit.
I am out of krazy glue.

But please do not mistake this
for a "my daddy wasn't there" poem; he was.
When my mother vanished in puff of crack smoke
my disabled brother and I ate cause he worked.
He made it possible for me to grow up
a middle-class black girl in a city where military money
made black kids think we were rich.

But somehow he forgot that princesses
never stop needing their daddies.
Though there was no wicked witch,
there was a Cinderella, and a very human stepmother
with fears of her own and a home that was not big enough
for the both us, and a father
that turned to a pillar of salt
because I kept on looking back.
Much like the millions of things in my life
I have ruined, I try not to think about that
but my daddy fought a lion for me last night.

And that does not seem remotely likely.
But lots of impossible shit has been happening as of late
and its starting to affect my sleep,

because on Tuesday of last week
I went to bed and woke up and a black man was president.
I went to bed last night and my daddy;
my daddy graduated from college a year after me,
married with two kids at the age of nineteen, daddy
was president in my crazy-ass dream.
There was no one in the White House but him and me.
Yet, this house wasn't built out of trembling dominoes or a
    deck of cards.
The chairs in this dream were hard and solid
like the foundation of two people who have finally
learned how to love each other. We talked.
We walked through the White House
exploring hidden rooms like a daddy and his daughter
watching cartoons when she was nine.
I was suddenly transported to a time when our relationship
was not a broken watch.

My father was a man, who knew me,
who loved me and showed me it was so
and I don't know why we were in the White House back yard
but we were having such a good time we must have been
    caught off guard
because a lion sprang out of no where and tried to attack.
But my daddy, y'all, my big, strong, presidential daddy
had my back. He fought that lion for me.
And I know this is just a dream and it may not make any sense.
But I have to tell you, that as of last Tuesday and ever since
something in me has shifted.
Perhaps you all missed it.

But two little girls who finally look like me
just might be in the White House playing hide-and-seek
with their daddy.
And I never thought that was plausible.
But tonight I am gonna call my father,
tell him I love him, believe he will return those words, and
     mean it.
Because today I am certain
anything is possible.

SALVAGED

All that is
sense, logic, reason
All that is order
that is basic
that is plain
as our whittled
down dreams
says
you are no
fairy dust
no last wish
no burning nova
in these palms

Says I should forget
this heat
this fire
given only to those
who have never carelessly
scorched their hands
by placing them too close
to your incinerator heart

Yet

All that is tendon
and bone

All that is
muscle, sinew, thumb
Know that you are
smoke
are flame
are cinder sweet
as breath

All that is fragile and foolish
in me
All that is reckless as
a child's mouth
welcomes this burn
Beckons whatever
devastation you carry with your wind
Woman

All that is left of these palms
is ash and I will
gladly
be scorched
bare earth
pinned beneath
the crackle
the sting

Whatever
remains after the fire
let me be that
Singed

Salvaged
Worth that much
more to
you
for having survived

AN EXCHANGE ON A TRAIN IN SPRING

The tears welling in her eyes are distant cousins
I will meet someday.
For now she is an amiable spy
who has overheard my joy;

knows my mother makes me laugh
out loud in quiet spaces; summons the sun in me.
This makes the woman on the train
smile like a somnolent moon.

"I wish I still had mine," she says.
Much like the slope of an unborn daughter's shoulder,
I know but cannot ever really know.

Not until my mother slips past my laugh
dances off the edge of all that allows me
to still see, hear, touch
her.

This fear will contract, release, and then
contract once more, before it is pulled
still born from my throat.
Until then, I am left with this.

It must be akin to losing
the most brilliant thought you will ever have

just before
it births itself into sound.

Forever you will wonder,
how it came to you,
why it left.
But mostly,
long desperately
to have it back.

ROBBIE Q. TELFER

DOUCHEBAG, *OR*
PSEUDO-FEMINIST HIPPIE DOUCHEBAG

A douche is a jet of water or chemicals
that a woman may shoot into her vagina
for many reasons.
Generally unhealthy,
douches destroy useful bacteria
that aid in the natural maintenance
of the vagina, leading to infection and
not significantly preventing pregnancy or
the spread of STDs.

A bag is a container of flexible material
with an opening at the top used for carrying things
like dream catchers,
like hookahs,
like pieces of shit
like you,
like you, sir, are a douchebag,
and I would like to be violent at you.

I see you back there
stalking the halls of women's
studies programs and the Whole
Foods olive bar just waiting
for the opportunity to bring up
What Would Gaia Do in a conversation,

just waiting for someone to notice
your 100% organic, free trade yoga ball.
Yes, douchebag, we are all impressed
by your mud chivalry.

Please,
please tell me about my aura.
Please tell me to be cool, man.
Please tell me about how many
misogynistic paper towel companies
you're currently boycotting.
Make sure you say it loud enough
for the ladies to hear.
Oh, please.

*Hey—loosen up! You'd be more receptive to this back rub if you
        opened your chakras!*

*Heeeey—I read that science and stuff has successfully generated
        sperm cells from bone, potentially making dudes obsolete!
        Can I touch your boob?*

Hey—I hate men. Wanna give me a blow-j?

You're not even trying anymore, douchebag!

I would like to talk about actual douches once more—
they are not new.
At the turn of the last century, some douches required
women to add a little bit of the liquid metal mercury into them

all in the fight against not-so-freshness.
My great-great aunt, Elsie Belle Wolling McCormac,
along with thousands of other shame-stalked women,
incorrectly measured the mercury
in her douche and died an excruciating death
as the metal obliterated her womb.

Do you know about control?
Can you see the connection at all?
There's a warning label on the box
but I don't think it's long enough for you.
The wicked tendrils of your soft
persuasion tearing at the wall
paper of someone else's room, you
pick-pocket, snake oil freighter,
fox in feathers waltzing freely
about the chicken coop.

Often a woman will employ the services
of a douche in order to cleanse herself
of blood, odor, semen. As it turns out,
the best way to accomplish this cleansing
is to let the vagina's unique microbial environment
do this work
itself.

To the perpetuators of shame, supplication,
and bacterial vaginosis, please,
give yourselves a shower, and let the vagina clean itself.
Just let it clean itself.

WHITE MEN OF MORTALITY VARIOUS

In the dream cafeteria my old postmodernism
professor Dr. B laughs with me about the famous poet
and his secret sexual misadventures with Muppets.
His current students laugh too but ours is knowing
laughter; theirs nervous, supine. Dr. B asks the kids if
they remember my bear poem and one blushes: I forgot
to bring my notes on Telfer. The assigned laughters fall.
Later outside the band practice rooms, an ex-girlfriend
begrudgingly announces the winner of the contest
inspired by the poem I wrote about my car. From the
crowd I yell to ensure she gets the make, model, color
right. Sometimes dreams are fucking easy to interpret.

Stanley Fish gave a lecture at my college and said
that postmodernism was bullshit (I'm paraphrasing)
and the actual Dr. B got on the Q&A mic to defend his
life the best he could. SF also said that if you're not an
expert in something you're basically bullshitting (I'm
not paraphrasing). He challenged everyone there to arm
wrestle his knowledge of John Milton. No one accepted.
Then he put on a striped singlet and spun a Model-T over
his head for an hour.

I wrote comic strip dialogue that goes:

Dumpy Guy: Man, if you don't think _____ is a total
hottie, you'd have to be blind, gay, and dead!

Sarcastic Animal: You'd be John Milton?

My friend said it wasn't a good comic strip because it essentially says *Hey! Look how much I know about John Milton!* He's right but I neglected to tell him that that's ALL I know about John Milton. I'm tired of saying John Milton. Maybe the *New Yorker* would like my comic strip about John Milton. John Milton.

Dr. B admitted once that he'd never read *Hamlet* and that at this point he'd probably not need to. I've read *Hamlet* but I don't have a word for the kind of reading that is saying the sentences in my head but actually thinking about how many girls I could have sex with if I had any game—that's how I read *Hamlet, Song of Myself,* and the first twenty pages of *Paradise Lost* by John Milton.

Harold Bloom discusses Hamlet like an old lover—one who he remembers fondly though briefly as if too much discussion will remind everyone that HB could have prevented the prince's death if he'da just kept his big ol' egghead outta all them books.

I've been accidentally recently publicly racist sexist I don't have a word for prejudice with good intentions.

When I ask the young poets I teach to define Poetry, their definitions widely variate alive polychromatic. They stop smiling and scribble when I tell them my definition. I wish I wrote what they define. I can't believe I corrected Erika when she said *Poetry is survival.*

It's hard to say what I mean when what I mean
is quicksand lightning bugs, I mean neighborhood
fragrances, I mean the birds who live in the airport, I
mean potato diseases and I don't know which ones, I mean
I don't know. I don't know what I mean. I'm basically
bullshitting.

You know?

BEAR BAITING

In Elizabethan England, a popular leisure activity was "bear baiting," a sport where a live bear with its teeth and claws filed down was presented in a coliseum, one of its legs secured to a stake in the ground. The bear would then be set upon by hunting dogs, with bets taken on the winner. The bears and dogs[1] would tear each other to pieces in front of jubilant onlookers, often amassed by the thousand.

Bear baiting was big business and much beloved by the populace. Theatres of the era, including Shakespeare's Globe, were forced to close on Thursdays to discourage splitting audience[2]. Even still, a Puritanical movement in the English parliament passed a law to outlaw bear baiting on Sundays—not for their horrendous cruelty to the animals, but rather because grandiose recreational activities were to be discouraged on a day supposedly devoted to worship. However, Queen Elizabeth I, a staunch advocate of bear baiting, overruled her Parliament's decision in favor of keeping the baiting arenas open on the Lord's Day. This unprecedented act ensured Elizabeth's immortal notoriety and earned her the additional title "Master Bear Baiter."

---

1   Dogs are the bear's closest biological relative.

2   To the status quo of the era, theatre and bear baiting were nearly interchangeable, two sides of the same amoral coin.

Now try not to judge Elizabeth or our forebears too harshly. It should be noted that in Elizabethan England, bears were plentiful; the Earth, newly round, and nature herself were infinite. So though cruel, it is universally enjoyable to witness the infinite conquered, symbolically and otherwise.

And think of our own descendants—future generations aghast (as you are now) at our attitudes toward water, oil, bananas, the polar ice caps, the Milky Way, and everything else in our world that is deceptively endless.

And think of the forebears of Elizabethan England; surely those Neanderthals passed on some vestigial terror that the eleven-foot-tall cave bears would one day capriciously extract them from their caves and mortal husks with a casual swipe of the paw.

How exhilarating it must have been to see fear destroyed like that.

Perhaps you are one of the very reasonable people; your metric for empathy and morality are perfectly calibrated so that right and wrong always sit on opposite sides of your mind, like boys and girls at an eighth grade dance. But entertain with me for a moment that you are not so reasonable; pretend that you're one of the evil boys; after all, a version of yourself, an analogue of who you are in this society—teacher, doctor, artist—sat in the bear baiting bleachers and let the spectacle fill them with joy. They were a community, anonymous as a theatre audience, boys and girls, laughter and cheers, dancing together.

Clearly, this is why bears in mainstream family culture vacillate between the humorous and the adorable—it is just a modern display of baiting. With every laugh these pages herein[3], every teddy bear clutched comfortingly close, every polar bear hawking Coca Cola, every Berenstein Bear exploit and foible, another mallet strike drives the stake down.

"Watch the big scary bear, Abigail. Isn't he dreadful? Watch him go down. He'll pay for being so dreadful."

However, besides commonplace huggable simulacra, the literal practice of bear baiting still goes on today in parts of Pakistan. Apparently they did not get the animal rights memo. Indeed, the impoverished masses of the third world are excessively challenged in the memo-getting department. They are still burdened with an authentic reality and its non-metonymic daily struggles. Burdened with real deserts[4]. Burdened with a real Mother Nature, with real teeth and claws who at any moment may capriciously remove them with a casual swipe of the paw.

---

[3]   There are at least five pieces regarding bears in this book, after all.

[4]   Not the desert of the real. Not the theatre. Not this desert theatre.

CLOWNS

There is a dark club full of hyenas
barking at an empty stage.

Jon Lovitz replaced Phil Hartman
on *News Radio* after one night when Andy
Dick fed cocaine to Phil Hartman's recently clean wife,
Brynn Hartman. Phil Hartman
told Brynn Hartman that if she started using again
he would leave her, so Brynn Hartman
shot Phil Hartman and herself in the head.
Years later, Andy
Dick taunted Jon Lovitz about how Andy
Dick caused Phil Hartman's death, so
Jon Lovitz grabbed Andy
Dick by the head and bounced his face off a
comedy club bar.

David Foster Wallace wrote a very simple and
easy to understand book called *Finite Jest*.
Richard Pryor burns. Gilda Radner smolders.
Andy Kaufman writhes on the ground with women.

Bill Hicks never gained mainstream popularity
because he couldn't tell more dick jokes than
jokes about the first Iraq War. Perpetually censored,
Bill Hicks was diagnosed with cancer,
taped a set on David Letterman, told more jokes
about abortion than the battle of the sexes.

David Letterman pulled the segment from the show,
and his friend Bill Hicks died a few months later.

Bill Cosby shot his shotgun mouth with a sleepy rage.
Michael Richards does the same but his pellets are flaccid.
Dave Chapelle walked away from millions of dollars
because he couldn't control WHY the hyenas were barking.

In February 2009, David Letterman aired the censored
Bill Hicks segment and publicly apologized to Bill Hicks'
mother, Mary Hicks. She only half-accepted the apology.

At Kermit the Frog's memorial service,
Miss Piggy had to run away from the podium
at the end of his eulogy. Scooter told the congregation
why we should live in the moment like Kermit did and then
Scooter died of AIDS just two years later. Big Bird
came out to sing "It's Not Easy Bein' Green" and for
a moment it sounded as if there was a human being
living inside of this giant yellow body, for a moment it
sounded like this impossible real person was starting to
crack and cry inside of this now trembling feathered body
all because a frog didn't want to bother people
by going to the hospital in time. Later, the ashes
of someone named Jim Henson were scattered
on a ranch in Santa Fe.

From the stage, you can't see the hyenas but
you can hear them barking. Your job is to be
meat dangling to tease out the barking. Your
job, clown, is to be meat dangling dance for the
canine scream that means that you're winning.

You're a failure if they think they can hear a real
human being shivering and frightened inside
your giant clown body. There's a two-drink
minimum, tip your waitress, you'll be here all night
you say, you'll be here all night sucking out
the cackles daring death to just try and take you.
And that's the joke, you know, life. Life is
a wonderful joke. When Tina Fey was five
years old, she was playing in her front yard,
a man walked up to her and just slashed her
across the face. When Stephen Colbert was
ten, his father and two oldest brothers died
in a plane crash on September 11th, 1974.
Mark Twain tried to swallow an entire planet's
imperialistic, selfish greed, stuff it inside
a funny white suit. Then the daughter of Samuel
Clemens died. Mark Twain kept working,
Samuel Clemens stopped working. We go
on, despite. Despite this, to spite this, in spite,
we go on. It really is a wonderful joke.
It's really quite hilarious.

BUDDY
WAKEFIELD

WE WERE EMERGENCIES

Let's think about what can go right tonight.
Receive what you believe.
No need to internalize the chaos.
It will still exist without you.
Take your hands off the controls.
We're all in this together.
Stop holding on with your neck so tight.
Tonight—
let your head climb back down through your throat
and into your body
so it can see the miracle it came here to be
so it can see you are not invisible.
Propellers just have a way of lookin' like that.
Some people see it. Some people don't.
Tonight I invite you
get out of your ghost
and see
we can stick anything into the fog
and make it look like a ghost
but tonight let us not become tragedies.
We are not funeral homes
with propane tanks in our windows
lookin' like cemeteries.
Cemeteries are just the Earth's way of not letting go.
Let go.
Tonight, poets, turn your stupid wrists

so far backwards
the razor blades in your pencil tips
can't get a good angle on all that beauty inside.
Step into this
with your airplane parts
move forward
and repeat after me with your heart:
I no longer need you to fuck me as hard as I hated myself.
Make love to me
like you know I am better than the worst thing I ever did.
Go slow.
I'm new to this
but I have seen nearly every city from a rooftop
without jumping.
I have realized that the moon
did not have to be full for us to love it
that we are not tragedies stranded here beneath it
that if my heart really broke every time I fell from love
I'd be able to offer you confetti by now.
But hearts don't break, y'all
they bruise and get better.
We were never tragedies.
We were emergencies.
You call 9-1-1.
Tell them I'm havin' a fantastic time.

HURLING CROWBIRDS AT MOCKINGBARS
(HOPE IS NOT A COURSE OF ACTION)

If we were created in God's image
then when God was a child
he smushed fire ants with his fingertips
and avoided tough questions.
There are ways around being the go-to person
even for ourselves
even when the answer is clear
like the holy water Gentiles drank
before they realized forgiveness
is the release of all hope for a better past.

I thought those were chime shells in your pocket
so I chucked a quarter at it
hoping to hear some part of you
respond on a high note.
You acted like I was hurling crowbirds at mockingbars
and abandoned me for not making sense.
Evidently, I don't experience things as rationally as you do.

For example, I know mercy
when I have enough money for the jukebox.
You understand the power of mercy
whenever someone shoves a stick of morphine
straight up into your heart.
It felt amazing
the days you were happy to see me

so I smashed a beehive against the ocean
to try and make our splash last longer.
Remember all the honey
had me lookin' like a jellyfish ape,
but you walked off the water in a porcupine of light
strands of gold
drizzled out to the tips of your wasps.
This is an apology letter to the both of us
for how long it took me to let things go.

It was not my intention to make such a
production of the emptiness between us
playing tuba on the tombstone of a soprano
to try and keep some dead singer's perspective alive.
It's just that I coulda swore you had sung me a love song
     back there
and that you meant it
but I guess sometimes people just chew with their mouth open

so I ate ear plugs alive with my throat
hoping they'd get lodged deep enough inside the empty spots
that I wouldn't have to hear you leaving
so I wouldn't have to listen to my heart keep saying
all my eggs were in a basket of red flags
all my eyes to a bucket of blindfolds
in the cupboard with the muzzles and the gauze
ya know I didn't mean to speed so far out and off
trying to drive all your nickels to the well
when you were happy to let them wishes fall

but I still show up for gentleman practice
in the company of lead dancers
hoping their grace will get stuck in my shoes.
Is that a handsome shadow on my breath, sweet woman
or is it a cattle call
in a school of fish? Still dance with me
less like a waltz for panic
more for the way we'd hoped to swing
the night we took off everything
and we were swingin' for the fences.

My love,
you know I wanna breathe deeper than this
you know I didn't mean to look so serious
didn't mean to act like a filthy floor
didn't mean to turn us both into a cutting board
but there were knives *stuck*
in the words where I came from
too much time in the back of my words.
I pulled knives from my back and my words.
I cut trombones from the moment you slipped away

and I know it left me lookin' like a knife fight, lady
yeah I know it left me feelin' like a shotgun shell
you know I know I mighta gone and lost my breath
but I wanna show ya how I found my breath
to death
it was buried under all the wind instruments
hidden in your castanets

goddamn—
if you ever wanna know how it felt when ya left
yeah if ya ever wanna come inside

just knock on the spot

where I finally pressed STOP

playing musical chairs with your exit signs.

Forgiveness
is for anyone who needs a safe passage through my mind.

I'm gonna cause you a miracle
when you see the way I kept God's image alive.

If I was really created in God's image
then when God was a boy
he wanted to grow up to be a man
a good man
and when God was a man
a good man
He started telling the truth in order to get honest
    responses.
He'd say,
"I know.
I really shoulda wore my cross
again
but I don't wanna scare the Gentiles off."

BAR FIGHT

I've been holding bar fights in my head
I could not possibly win.
But I do.
I do win.

JEAN HEATH

In the end
Jean Heath's home was filled with people
who claimed to know her better than they actually did.
They swapped tissues and embellished stories
to appear closer to Jean Heath than they actually were
in the same way wearing expensive clothes on Sunday
apparently brings wealthy Baptists closer to God than
    they actually are.

It were mostly unfamiliar faces
who seemed to be looking for due credit
on the role they may or may not have played
in the life of Jean Heath
networking their sorrow and searching
like they always do in every death
for the gate to restoration.
As if this life really wants us to stay here.

They took turns crying over Jean Heath's face
as a sign that she would be missed.
There was so much crying that I, the caregiver,
could hear Jean Heath's bed sheets slap together when she moved
and there was food, y'all
holy holy there was so much food.
At least an acre of it.
Across the kitchen countertops and over the tables

falling out of the refrigerator and along the arms of chairs
there were plastic cups with names written on them
sometimes twice. Sometimes two cups.
Kids lose shit.

There was ambrosia with snot on it
cornbread with tears in it
black-eyed peas with the trembling ladle
strawberry rhubarbed wire pie, melty vanilla ice cream pulp
and there were perfect middle squares still left in the brownie pan.
I know who ate the end pieces.
The little ones
were warned
that death is a very serious matter
so they had better not act up
or else they would be forced
to pick their own switch
and get whipped with it.

We were tricked into fearing the ways we will leave this planet.

Emily Beeshold was 26 years old that day when she
came to play piano for her best friend Jean Heath, age 87
who lay flat and velvet on her death bed
lookin' like the front pew of a gospel church without the guilt.
When the other guests asked Emily how she knew Jean Heath
Emily thought of Jean's lonely days on the porch
when no one came to visit
when the money ran out
when the yearning for love haunted her

taught her how heavy the hollows are
how crippled a memory can make ya
how sometimes she'd cry so hard her throat locked out all
    the noise.
I trust you people…
about as far as I can throw you
Emily said
and I can't throw you.

The candles inside her piano keys
are why Emily's fingertips burn when she plays.
She doesn't scare Jean Heath when she plays like that.
She bangs both feet down on the sustain pedal bouncing
when she sings like that
teeth all gripped out like a hallway howling
Holler holler she sang
I'm goin' home.
Might be a little bit bit but
I'm gonna show 'em.
Might be dirty
might be skinny like water
but there's a hole in God and I'm not
gonna fall down in there.

And that day when she played
sometimes with her knuckles
mostly with her memory
she remembered a true story she read alone
in a book about self acceptance
where a daughter sits next to her mother in a coma
until one morning before dawn

the mother wakes up
looks very clearly and very intently at her daughter
and says, *You know,*
my whole life
I thought something was wrong with me.
Then the mother shook her own head as if to say *what a waste*
before she slipped back into her coma
and died several hours later.
You knew she would.

These stories we give each other
they're just different reasons for begging you to stay
but nobody's gonna stay here.
Emily knows Jean Heath won't stay.
She's cool with that.
They both just wished they would've known a little sooner
about this life that every loss
doesn't have to cost so much
doesn't have to hit so heavy
doesn't have to get so dirty

dirty dirty like Christ
on his little brown mule.
I was baptized in tap water
and I never really went to school.
I got a hunger for ya.
I got a hunger for you
but I never but I never
but I never woulda ever let it
hurt you.

Jean Heath was tender and bossy in the moment
she finally called Emily Beeshold to her bedside.
While Jean was happy that her home
smelled like a baked good
and she was thankful
for the best of the gestures from the guests in the bedrooms
and she was wondering about some of the recipes,
Jean was very clear and very intent
when she finally pulled Emily's ear
down to her mouth and said inside of it,

Get these people out of my house.
I've never died before
and I'm gonna enjoy it.

KIT WALLACH

DIRECTIONS

Let's suppose, for arguments sake,
that you and I went to the zoo.
And while we were in front of the cage
with the three-toed sloth—who,
it turns out, is a very agile swimmer,
and can grow to be up to six feet long—
let's suppose that while we stood
in front of this great organic monument
to furry inertia and a deep, abiding
respect for how slowly the earth turns,
I looked over at your face and realized
that what we were on was a date,
which explained why we were holding hands,
and not talking very much,
and why I was suddenly having a harder time
acting like a human being than
the monkeys in the monkey cage—
let's say I found myself suddenly colder-blooded
than all of the snakes they keep behind glass
in that funny room with the low light and the palm fronds—
it wouldn't be your fault.

If that were to happen, though, I have some advice.
Take me to the penguins.
Take me to the penguins, and I will turn back
into your friend, who likes things, and thinks you're cute,

and thinks the penguins are great,
and is happy to be at the zoo with you.
Take me to that ridiculous swimming pool
they have set up, with the concrete slides,
and the little black and white penguin-citizens
having decent, responsible playtime
in and out of the cold, cold water—
I will recover my wits if you take me to where
they keep the flightless birds shaped like small eggplants,
who manage to look noble, somehow,
as they navigate their clearly pointless lives,
and eat fish, and dive in the water, and
push each other off their little concrete islands,
in a way that reminds me of junior high school boys,
and makes me think maybe I shouldn't care
very much about what is romantic and what isn't—

JOHNNY APPLESEED

Come all you fair and tender ladies,
Be careful how you court young men…

I
More important than the footprints
he left in the new dark earth
was the way the soles of his feet looked
as he lifted them:
the walking,
the leaving,
the little he had,
that he was always alone.

We loved him for the figure he cut
against the low horizon—
sky burning orange behind him, his
tin cup silhouette.

II
Johnny is not named Appletree.
Apple seed, wooden teardrop lying still
in the snow cave of apple flesh.

The teeth of the world rip at the skin
thin as the breathing in your back,
thin as the air that comes through the window casings.

The lips and teeth of the world crush
the meat of the apple into drift ice.

But apple seed, you and your brothers lie still as the
five points of a star, rocking gently
in your apple cradles,
deep within the eating apple—
if the teeth of the world ever reach you, well,
the tongue would just spit you back out.

III
A young woman, a farmer's wife,
kneads the knuckles of her hands in the folds of her apron,
and looks out the window to see
Johnny, patron saint of introduced species,
of strangers, of men who dream of raising
red mountains from the broad swell of the plains.

He is just leaving. The pan on his head
makes him look like a poorly-equipped soldier.
As he walks,
his hands drip seeds.
They form a dotted line on the map of his travels.

A hundred years pass.
The trees have become, in spring, old
Japanese men; in summer, green fruit hangs heavy as
    earlobes,
and in the fall, an apple with a bloom of red
on its spotted skin transfers from a low branch

to the palm of a child, who later that day
will feed it to a mare with soft lips
and wet nostrils, and when she nuzzles his hand
he will feel, wondering, his first true moment of human
inadequacy—and the horse and the tree are the same
stooping creature; gentle with the child,
looking him in the eye like a lover.

And in the old apple trees lining the road
we see nothing left of Johnny, save maybe
that look of exposure to the elements, and perhaps
one long, soft kiss he might have shared
with a farmer's wife, before he remembered
he wasn't any good at talking to people, and moved
quietly along down the land, his pockets always full.

A BRIEF MILITARY HISTORY

She's all legs in the back.
She's long and tall and
her skirt is shorter than God's temper.
The pavement licks at her heels as she walks—
she's locomotive; she's train.

You drive by slow and
she moves sexy, sexy; it happens
just the way they showed you:
walking and driving getting twisted up
in bass beats along the sidewalk—
between the glimmer of the streetlight
and the cheap edge of her swaying hip,
the stone of the curb gets blurry.

The stoplights turn red and green;
the headlights beam, blink break lights in the rain.

In ancient cultures they prayed to big god-people
and shot animals with sharpened pieces of stone. Then,
we got careless with our money;
we traded up to guns and went hunting for each other,
we called it fancy names.
We threw big parties,
bigger empires—
still,

this woman, with the too much hair on her head
and the leather body armor with strategic holes—
this woman with the boots done up and the flesh stuck out,
this woman with the face you can't see,
with the lungs buried under her lace and skin—
her drawn outline would look so good
on your caveman-wall; her body
would make a beautiful rug
tacked down to your stone bed;

you could make a nice loud noise with this woman.
You could make a loud noise into her all night, until the sound
came out her own mouth and the moon caught
in the bare branches of the tree outside your window, and then
everyone would know what kind of a man you are,
when you wore her, tied, slung across your body
to the next big fire.

This is your grand conquest.
Your weapon-given right.

You'd better get on that.

BEHOLD THE NOTHING THAT IS NOT THERE

You bend the sundae spoon like a note on a slide guitar, and
I listen, looking up from under your eyes,
as they roll over the Formica tabletop, up the chrome
   napkin holder,
rest out the window.

So much noise and light, menus in this generic restaurant,
so many golden-fried edges of things: potatoes, leaking
   onion rings—
I can almost see the little ball of thought spinning between us,
like a ripened apple still spinning on its branch.

Things would be different
if I were one of those girls who knew how to tie
maraschino cherry stems with her tongue,
big white teeth and lip-liner, eyes like full milk pails.
If I were one of those girls who knew when to laugh,
instead of always looking for something funny to say myself.

They are not looking
for an arm with freckles to memorize;
they are not looking for a space
between shoulders that smells of opened pears;
they are never in the market for hair follicles set misaligned,
ragged cattail teeth, mouth like a leather purse.

You are much too much like me: the way you tear through
sugar packets like tubes of glitter-paint, lining up the refuse
into little, wet-suitcase stairways.

We are a piece of work. Someday they'll take all of our
wrong angles, and make wire hangers of us—
we'll dangle like convicts on department store racks,
and other, more expensive women will pick me out from
under their new lace negligees, and some catalogue model
of a man will wear a sweater off your elbows, and they
will both be much, much better than us at all of this.

OTHER GREAT WRITE BLOODY BOOKS

THE GOOD THINGS ABOUT AMERICA
An illustrated, un-cynical look at our American Landscape. Various authors.
Edited by Kevin Staniec and Derrick Brown

JUNKYARD GHOST REVIVAL
with Andrea Gibson, Buddy Wakefield, Anis Mojgani, Derrick Brown, Robbie Q,
Sonya Renee and Cristin O'keefe Aptowicz

THE LAST AMERICAN VALENTINE:
ILLUSTRATED POEMS TO SEDUCE AND DESTROY
24 authors, 12 illustrators team up for a collection of non-sappy love poetry
Edited by Derrick Brown

SOLOMON SPARROWS ELECTRIC WHALE REVIVAL
Poetry Compilation by Buddy Wakefield, Anis Mojgani, Derrick Brown, Dan
Leamen & Mike McGee

THE ELEPHANT ENGINE HIGH DIVE REVIVAL
Anthology

STEVE ABEE, GREAT BALLS OF FLOWERS (2009)
New Poems by Steve Abee

SCANDALABRA
New poetry compilation by Derrick Brown

I LOVE YOU IS BACK
Poetry compilation (2004-2006) by Derrick Brown

BORN IN THE YEAR OF THE BUTTERFLY KNIFE
Poetry anthology, 1994-2004 by Derrick Brown

DON'T SMELL THE FLOSS
New Short Fiction Pieces by Matty Byloos

THE CONSTANT VELOCITY OF TRAINS
New Poems by Lea Deschenes

HEAVY LEAD BIRDSONG
New Poems by Ryler Dustin

UNCONTROLLED EXPERIMENTS IN FREEDOM
New Poems by Brian Ellis
LETTING MYSELF GO